ENGLISH PROSE

A SERIES OF RELATED ESSAYS FOR THE DISCUSSION AND PRACTICE OF THE ART OF WRITING

SELECTED AND EDITED

BY

GEORGE ROY ELLIOTT,

PREFACE

The selections in the present volume, designed primarily for the discussion and practice in college classes of the art of composition, have been arranged under a scheme which the editors believe to be new. There are nine related groups. Each successive group represents a different phase of life, beginning with character and personality, and concluding with art and literature. The whole together, as the table of contents will show, thus presents a body of ideas that includes practically all the great departments of human thought and interest.

It is evident that certain ideals of teaching composition underlie the scheme. The editors believe heartily with Pater that "the chief stimulus of good style is to possess a full, rich, complex matter to grapple with". Instruction in writing, it is to be feared, too often neglects this sound doctrine and places an emphasis upon formal matters that seems disproportionate, especially when form is made to appear as a thing apart. Form and content go together and one must not suffer at the expense of the other. But a sustained interest in the ways and means of correct expression is aroused only when the student feels that he has something to express. Instructors often contend indeed that the ideas of undergraduates are far to seek, and that most of the time in the class-room is therefore best spent upon formal exercises and drill. The editors do not share this view. They believe that there is no class of people more responsive to new ideas and impressions than college students, and none more eager, when normally stimulated, to express themselves in writing. They have therefore aimed to present a series of related selections that would arouse thought and provoke oral discussion in the class-room, as well as furnish suitable models of style. In most cases the pieces are too long to be adequately handled in one class hour. A live topic may well be discussed for several hours, until its various sides have been examined and students are awakened to the many questions at issue. The editors have aimed, also, to supply selections so rich and vital in content that instructors themselves will feel challenged to add to the class discussion from their own knowledge and experience, and so turn a stream of fresh ideas upon "stock notions". Thus English composition, which in many courses in our larger institutions is now almost the only non-special study, can be made a direct means of liberalization in the meaning and art of life, as well as an instrument for correct and effective writing.

The present volume therefore differs from others in the same field. Many recent collections contain pieces too short and unrelated to satisfy the ideals suggested above—ideals which, the editors feel sure, are held by an increasing number of teachers. And older and newer collections alike have been constructed primarily with the purpose of illustrating the conventional categories,—description, narration, exposition. Teachers of composition everywhere are becoming distrustful of an arrangement which is frankly at variance with the actual practice of writing, and are of the opinion that it is better to set the student to the task of composition without confining him too narrowly to one form of discourse. The editors have deliberately avoided, however, the other extreme, which is reflected in one or two recent volumes, of choosing pieces of one type to the exclusion of all others. In collections of this kind variety in form and subject-matter is fully as important as richness of content. Instructors who believe in the use of the types of discourse as the most practicable means of instruction, will find all the types liberally represented in the present volume. And in order to meet their requirements even more adequately, the editors have included two short stories at the end, as examples of narration with a plot.

Much attention has been given to the suggestions at the end of the volume with the aim of making them practically serviceable and, at the same time, as free as possible from duplication of class work. This aim, the editors came to believe, could best be attained by providing for each group of selections definite suggestions of theme-subjects to be derived by the student from supplementary readings closely related to that group.

CONTENTS

I. THE PERSONAL LIFE.

1. Self-Reliance...............RALPH WALDO EMERSON

2. Early Education
   at Herne Hill............JOHN RUSKIN

3. A Crisis in My
   Mental History............JOHN STUART MILL

4. Old China..................CHARLES LAMB

II. EDUCATION.

5. What is Education?..........THOMAS HENRY HUXLEY

6. Knowledge Viewed in Relation to Learning .....JOHN HENRY NEWMAN

7. Literature and Science......MATTHEW ARNOLD

8. How to Read...............FREDERIC HARRISON

III. RECREATION AND TRAVELS.

9. On Going a Journey..........WILLIAM HAZLITT

10. Regrets of a Mountaineer....LESLIE STEPHEN

IV. SOCIAL LIFE AND MANNERS.

11. Behavior..................RALPH WALDO EMERSON

12. Manners and Fashion.........HERBERT SPENCER

SELF-RELIANCE[1]

RALPH WALDO EMERSON

I read the other day some verses written by an eminent painter which were original and not conventional. Always the soul hears an admonition in such lines, let the subject be what it may. The sentiment they instil is of more value than any thought they may contain. To believe your own thought, to believe that what is true for you in your private heart is true for all men,—that is genius. Speak your latent conviction, and it shall be the universal sense; for always the inmost becomes the outmost—and our first thought is rendered back to us by the trumpets of the Last Judgment. Familiar as the voice of the mind is to each, the highest merit we ascribe to Moses, Plato and Milton is that they set at naught books and traditions, and spoke not what men, but what they thought. A man should learn to detect and watch that gleam of light which flashes across his mind from within, more than the luster of the firmament of bards and sages. Yet he dismisses without notice his thought, because it is his. In every work of genius we recognize our own rejected thoughts; they come back to us with a certain alienated majesty. Great works of art have no more affecting lesson for us than this. They teach us to abide by our spontaneous impression with good-humored inflexibility then most when the whole cry of voices is on the other side. Else to-morrow a stranger will say with masterly good sense precisely what we have thought and felt all the time, and we shall be forced to take with shame our own opinion from another.

There is a time in every man's education when he arrives at the conviction that envy is ignorance; that imitation is suicide; that he must take himself for better for worse as his portion; that though the wide universe is full of good, no kernel of nourishing corn can come to him but through his toil bestowed on that plot of ground which is given to him to till. The power which resides in him is new in nature, and none but he knows what that is which he can do, nor does he know until he has tried. Not for nothing one face, one character, one fact, makes much impression on him, and another none. It is not without preestablished harmony, this sculpture in the memory. The eye was placed where one ray should fall, that it might testify of that particular ray. Bravely let him speak the utmost syllable of his confession. We but half express ourselves, and are ashamed of that divine idea which each of us represents. It may be safely trusted as proportionate and of good issues, so it be faithfully imparted, but God will not have his work made manifest by cowards. It needs a divine man to exhibit anything divine. A man is relieved and gay when he has put his heart into his work and done his best; but what he has said or done otherwise shall give him no peace. It is a deliverance which does not deliver. In the attempt his genius deserts him; no muse befriends; no invention, no hope.

Trust thyself: every heart vibrates to that iron string. Accept the place the divine providence has found for you, the society of your contemporaries, the connection of events. Great men have always done so, and confided themselves childlike to the genius of their age, betraying their perception that the Eternal was stirring at their heart, working through their hands, predominating in all their being. And we are now men, and must accept in the highest mind the same transcendent destiny; and not pinched in a corner, not cowards fleeing before a revolution, but redeemers and benefactors, pious aspirants to be noble clay under the Almighty effort let us advance on Chaos and the Dark.

What pretty oracles nature yields us on this text in the face and behavior of children, babes, and even brutes. That divided and rebel mind, that distrust of a sentiment because our arithmetic has computed the strength and means opposed to our purpose, these have not. Their mind being whole, their eye is as yet unconquered, and when we look in their faces, we are disconcerted. Infancy conforms to nobody; all conform to it; so that one babe commonly makes four or five out of the adults who prattle and play to it. So God has armed youth and puberty and manhood no less with its own piquancy and charm, and made it enviable and gracious and its claims not to be put by, if it will stand by itself. Do not think the youth has no force, because he cannot speak to you and me. Hark! in the next room who spoke so clear and emphatic? Good Heaven! it is he! it is that very lump of bashfulness and phlegm which for weeks has done nothing but eat when you were by, and now rolls out these words like bell-strokes. It seems he knows how to speak to his contemporaries. Bashful or bold then, he will know how to make us seniors very unnecessary.

The nonchalance of boys who are sure of a dinner, and would disdain as much as a lord to do or say aught to conciliate one, is the healthy attitude of human nature. How is a boy the master of society!—independent, irresponsible, looking out from his corner on such people and facts as pass by, he tries and sentences them on their merits, in the swift, summary way of boys, as good, bad, interesting, silly, eloquent, troublesome. He cumbers himself never about consequences, about interests; he gives an independent, genuine verdict. You must court him; he does not court you. But the man is as it were clapped into jail by his consciousness. As soon as he has once acted or spoken with éclat he is a committed person, watched by the sympathy or the hatred of hundreds, whose affections must now enter into his account. There is no Lethe for this. Ah, that he could pass again into his neutral, godlike independence! Who can thus lose all pledge and, having observed, observe again from the same unaffected, unbiased, unbribable, unaffrighted innocence, must always be formidable, must always engage the poet's and the man's regards. Of such an immortal youth the force would be felt. He would utter opinions on all passing affairs, which being seen to be not private but necessary, would sink like darts into the ear of men and put them in fear.

These are the voices which we hear in solitude, but they grow faint and inaudible as we enter into the world. Society everywhere is in conspiracy against the manhood of every one of its members. Society is a joint-stock company, in which the members agree, for the better securing of his bread to each shareholder, to surrender the liberty and culture of the eater. The virtue in most request is conformity. Self-reliance is its aversion. It loves not realities and creators, but names and customs.

Whoso would be a man, must be a nonconformist. He who would gather immortal palms must not be hindered by the name of goodness, but must explore if it be goodness. Nothing is at last sacred but the integrity of our own mind. Absolve you to yourself, and you shall have the suffrage of the world. I remember an answer which when quite young I was prompted to make to a valued adviser who was wont to importune me with the deaf old doctrines of the church. On my saying, What have I to do with the sacredness of traditions, if I live wholly from within? my friend suggested, —"But these impulses may be from below, not from above." I replied, "They do not seem to me to be such; but if I am the devil's child, I will live then from the devil." No law can be sacred to me but that of my nature. Good and bad are but names very readily transferable to that or this; the only right is what is after my constitution; the only wrong what is against it. A man is to carry himself in the presence of all opposition as if every thing were titular and ephemeral but he. I am ashamed to think how easily we capitulate to badges and names, to large societies and dead institutions. Every decent and well-spoken individual affects and sways me more than is right. I ought to go upright and vital, and speak the rude truth in all ways. If malice and vanity wear the coat of philanthropy, shall that pass? If an angry bigot assumes this bountiful cause of Abolition, and comes to me with his last news from Barbadoes, why should I not say to him, "Go love thy infant; love thy wood-chopper; be good-natured and modest; have that grace; and never varnish your hard, uncharitable ambition with this incredible tenderness for black folk a thousand miles off. Thy love afar is spite at home." Rough and graceless would be such greeting, but truth is handsomer than the affectation of love. Your goodness must have some edge to it,— else it is none. The doctrine of hatred must be preached, as the counteraction of the doctrine of love, when that pules and whines. I shun father and mother and wife and brother when my genius calls me. I would write on the lintels of the door-post, *Whim*. I hope it is somewhat better than whim at last, but we cannot spend the day in explanation. Expect me not to show cause why I seek or why I exclude company. Then, again, do not tell me, as a good man did to-day, of my obligation to put all poor men in good situations. Are they *my* poor? I tell thee, thou foolish philanthropist, that I grudge the dollar, the dime, the cent I give to such men as do not belong to me and to whom I do not belong. There is a class of persons to whom by all spiritual affinity I am bought and sold; for them I will go to prison if need be; but your miscellaneous popular charities; the education at college of fools; the building of meeting-houses to the vain end to which many now stand; alms to sots, and the thousandfold Relief Societies;—though I confess with shame I sometimes succumb and give the dollar, it is a wicked dollar, which by-and-by I shall have the manhood to withhold.

Virtues are, in the popular estimate, rather the exception than the rule. There is the man *and* his virtues. Men do what is called a good action, as some piece of courage or charity, much as they would pay a fine in expiation of daily non-appearance on parade. Their works are done as an apology or extenuation of their living in the world,—as invalids and the insane pay a high board. Their virtues are penances. I do not wish to expiate, but to live. My life is not an apology, but a life. It is for itself and not for a spectacle. I much prefer that it should be of a lower strain, so it be genuine and equal, than that it should be glittering and unsteady. I wish it to be sound and sweet, and not to need diet and bleeding. My life should be unique; it should be an alms, a battle, a conquest, a medicine. I ask primary evidence that you are a man, and refuse this appeal from the man to his actions. I know that for myself it makes no difference whether I do or forbear those actions which are reckoned excellent. I cannot consent to pay for a privilege where I have intrinsic right. Few and mean as my gifts may be, I actually am, and do not need for my own assurance or the assurance of my fellows any secondary testimony.

What I must do is all that concerns me, not what the people think. This rule, equally arduous in actual and in intellectual life, may serve for the whole distinction between greatness and meanness. It is the harder because you will always find those who think they know what is your duty better than you know it. It is easy in the world to live after the world's opinion; it is easy in solitude to live after our own; but the great man is he who in the midst of the crowd keeps with perfect sweetness the independence of solitude.

The objection to conforming to usages that have become dead to you is that it scatters your force. It loses your time and blurs the impression of your character. If you maintain a dead church, contribute to a dead Bible Society, vote with a great party either for the Government or against it, spread your table like base housekeepers,—under all these screens I have difficulty to detect the precise man you are. And of course so much force is withdrawn from your proper life. But do your thing, and I shall know you. Do your work, and you shall reinforce yourself. A man must consider what a blindman's-bluff is this game of conformity. If I know your sect I anticipate your argument. I hear a preacher announce for his text and topic the expediency of one of the institutions of his church. Do I not know beforehand that not possibly can he say a new and spontaneous word? Do I not know that with all this ostentation of examining the grounds of the institution he will do no such thing? Do I not know that he is pledged to himself not to look but at one side, the permitted side, not as a man, but as a parish minister? He is a retained attorney, and these airs of the bench are the emptiest affectation. Well, most men have bound their eyes with one or another handkerchief, and attached themselves to some one of these communities of opinion. This conformity makes them not false in a few particulars, authors of a few lies, but false in all particulars. Their every truth is not quite true. Their two is not the real two, their four not the real four: so that every word they say chagrins us and we know not where to begin to set them right. Meantime nature is not slow to equip us in the prison-uniform of the party to which we adhere. We come to wear one cut of face and figure, and acquire by degrees the gentlest asinine expression. There is a mortifying experience in particular, which does not fail to wreak itself also in the general history; I mean "the foolish face of praise," the forced smile which we put on in company where we do not feel at ease, in answer to conversation which does not interest us. The muscles, not spontaneously moved but moved by a low usurping wilfulness, grow tight about the outline of the face, and make the most disagreeable sensation; a sensation of rebuke and warning which no brave young man will suffer twice.

For non-conformity the world whips you with its displeasure. And therefore a man must know how to estimate a sour face. The bystanders look askance on him in the public street or in the friend's parlor. If this aversation had its origin in contempt and resistance like his own he might well go home with a sad countenance; but the sour faces of the multitude, like their sweet faces, have no deep cause,—disguise no god, but are put on and off as the wind blows and a newspaper directs. Yet is the discontent of the multitude more formidable than that of the senate and the college. It is easy enough for a firm man who knows the world to brook the rage of the cultivated classes. Their rage is decorous and prudent, for they are timid, as being very vulnerable themselves. But when to their feminine rage the indignation of the people is added, when the ignorant and the poor are aroused, when the unintelligent brute force that lies at the bottom of society is made to growl and mow, it needs the habit of magnanimity and religion to treat it godlike as a trifle of no concernment.

The other terror that scares us from self-trust is our consistency; a reverence for our past act or word because the eyes of others have no other data for computing our orbit than our past acts, and we are loath to disappoint them.

But why should you keep your head over your shoulder? Why drag about this monstrous corpse of your memory, lest you contradict somewhat you have stated in this or that public place? Suppose you should contradict yourself; what then? It seems to be a rule of wisdom never to rely on your memory alone, scarcely even in acts of pure memory, but to bring the past for judgment into the thousand-eyed present, and live ever in a new day. Trust your emotion. In your metaphysics you have denied personality to the Deity, yet when the devout motions of the soul come, yield to them heart and life, though they should clothe God with shape and color. Leave your theory, as Joseph his coat in the hand of the harlot, and flee.

A foolish consistency is the hobgoblin of little minds, adored by little statesmen and philosophers and divines. With consistency a great soul has simply nothing to do. He may as well concern himself with his shadow on the wall. Out upon your guarded lips! Sew them up with packthread, do. Else if you would be a man speak what you think to-day in words as hard as cannon balls, and to-morrow speak what to-morrow thinks in hard words again, though it contradict every thing you said to-day. Ah, then, exclaim the aged ladies, you shall be sure to be misunderstood! Misunderstood! It is a right fool's word. Is it so bad then to be misunderstood? Pythagoras was misunderstood, and Socrates, and Jesus, and Luther, and Copernicus, and Galileo, and Newton, and every pure and wise spirit that ever took flesh. To be great is to be misunderstood.

I suppose no man can violate his nature. All the sallies of his will are rounded in by the law of his being, as the inequalities of Andes and Himmaleh are insignificant in the curve of the sphere. Nor does it matter how you gauge and try him. A character is like an acrostic or Alexandrian stanza;—read it forward, backward, or across, it still spells the same thing. In this pleasing contrite wood-life which God allows me, let me record day by day my honest thought without prospect or retrospect, and, I cannot doubt, it will be found symmetrical, though I mean it not and see it not. My book should smell of pines and resound with the hum of insects. The swallow over my window should interweave that thread or straw he carries in his bill into my web also. We pass for what we are. Character teaches above our wills. Men imagine that they communicate their virtue or vice only by overt actions, and do not see that virtue or vice emit a breath every moment.

Fear never but you shall be consistent in whatever variety of actions, so they be each honest and natural in their hour. For of one will, the actions will be harmonious, however unlike they seem. These varieties are lost sight of when seen at a little distance, at a little height of thought. One tendency unites them all. The voyage of the best ship is a zigzag line of a hundred tacks. This is only microscopic criticism. See the line from a sufficient distance, and it straightens itself to the average tendency. Your genuine action will explain itself and will explain your other genuine actions. Your conformity explains nothing. Act singly, and what you have already done singly will justify you now. Greatness always appeals to the future. If I can be great enough now to do right and scorn eyes, I must have done so much right before as to defend me now. Be it how it will, do right now. Always scorn appearances and you always may. The force of character is cumulative. All the foregone days of virtue work their health into this. What makes the majesty of the heroes of the senate and the field, which so fills the imagination? The consciousness of a train of great days and victories behind. There they all stand and shed an united light on the advancing actor. He is attended as by a visible escort of angels to every man's eye. That is it which throws thunder into Chatham's voice, and dignity into Washington's port, and America into Adams's eye. Honor is venerable to us because it is no ephemeris. It is always ancient virtue. We worship it to-day because it is not of to-day. We love it and pay it homage because it is not a trap for our love and homage, but is self-dependent, self-derived, and therefore of an old immaculate pedigree, even if shown in a young person.

I hope in these days we have heard the last of conformity and consistency. Let the words be gazetted and ridiculous henceforward. Instead of the gong for dinner, let us hear a whistle from the Spartan fife. Let us bow and apologize never more. A great man is coming to eat at my house. I do not wish to please him; I wish that he should wish to please me. I will stand here for humanity, and though I would make it kind, I would make it true. Let us affront and reprimand the smooth mediocrity and squalid contentment of the times, and hurl in the face of custom and trade and office, the fact which is the upshot of all history, that there is a great responsible Thinker and Actor moving wherever moves a man; that a true man belongs to no other time or place, but is the center of things. Where he is, there is nature. He measures you and all men and all events. You are constrained to accept his standard. Ordinarily, every body in society reminds us of somewhat else, or of some other person. Character, reality, reminds you of nothing else; it takes place of the whole creation. The man must be so much that he must make all circumstances indifferent—put all means into the shade. This: all great men are and do. Every true man is a cause, a country, and an age; requires infinite spaces and numbers and time fully to accomplish his thought;—and posterity seem to follow his steps as a procession. A man Caesar is born, and for ages after we have a Roman Empire. Christ is born, and millions of minds so grow and cleave to his genius that he is confounded with virtue and the possible of man. An institution is the lengthened shadow of one man; as, the Reformation, of Luther; Quakerism, of Fox; Methodism, of Wesley; Abolition, of Clarkson. Scipio, Milton called "the height of Rome;" and all history resolves itself very easily into the biography of a few stout and earnest persons.

Let a man then know his worth, and keep things under his feet. Let him not peep or steal, or skulk up and down with the air of a charity-boy, a bastard, or an interloper in the world which exists for him. But the man in the street, finding no worth in himself which corresponds to the force which built a tower or sculptured a marble god, feels poor when he looks on these. To him a palace, a statue, or a costly book has an alien and forbidding air, much like a gay equipage, and seems to say like that, "Who are you, sir?" Yet they all are his, suitors for his notice, petitioners to his faculties that they will come out and take possession. The picture waits for my verdict; it is not to command me, but I am to settle its claim to praise. That popular fable of the sot who was picked up dead drunk in the street, carried to the duke's house, washed and dressed and laid in the duke's bed, and, on his waking, treated with all obsequious ceremony like the duke, and assured that he had been insane—owes its popularity to the fact that it symbolizes so well the state of man, who is in the world a sort of sot, but now and then wakes up, exercises his reason and finds himself a true prince.

Our reading is mendicant and sycophantic. In history our imagination makes fools of us, plays us false. Kingdom and lordship, power and estate, are a gaudier vocabulary than private John and Edward in a small house and common day's work: but the things of life are the same to both: the sum total of both is the same. Why all this deference to Alfred and Scanderbeg and Gustavus? Suppose they were virtuous; did they wear out virtue? As great a stake depends on your private act to-day as followed their public and renowned steps. When private men shall act with original views, the luster will be transferred from the actions of kings to those of gentlemen.

The world has indeed been instructed by its kings, who have so magnetized the eyes of nations. It has been taught by this colossal symbol the mutual reverence that is due from man to man. The joyful loyalty with which men have everywhere suffered the king, the noble, or the great proprietor to walk among them, by a law of his own, make his own scale of men and things and reverse theirs, pay for benefits not with money but with honor, and represent the Law in his person, was the hieroglyphic by which they obscurely signified their consciousness of their own right and comeliness, the right of every man.

The magnetism which all original action exerts is explained when we inquire the reason of self-trust. Who is the Trustee? What is the aboriginal Self, on which a universal reliance may be grounded? What is the nature and power of that science-baffling star, without parallax, without calculable elements, which shoots a ray of beauty even into trivial and impure actions, if the least mark of independence appear? The inquiry leads us to that source, at once the essence of genius, the essence of virtue, and the essence of life, which we call Spontaneity or Instinct. We denote this primary wisdom as Intuition, whilst all later teachings are tuitions. In that deep force, the last fact behind which analysis cannot go, all things find their common origin. For the sense of being which in calm hours rises, we know not how, in the soul, is not diverse from things, from space, from light, from time, from man, but one with them and proceedeth obviously from the same source whence their life and being also proceedeth. We first share the life by which things exist and afterward see them as appearances in nature and forget that we have shared their cause. Here is the fountain of action and the fountain of thought. Here are the lungs of that inspiration which giveth man wisdom, of that inspiration of man which cannot be denied without impiety and atheism. We lie in the lap of immense intelligence, which makes us organs of its activity and receivers of its truth. When we discern justice, when we discern truth, we do nothing of ourselves, but allow a passage to its beams. If we ask whence this comes, if we seek to pry into the soul that causes—all metaphysics, all philosophy is at fault. Its presence or its absence is all we can affirm. Every man discerns between the voluntary acts of his mind and his involuntary perceptions. And to his involuntary perceptions: he knows a perfect respect is due. He may err in the expression of them, but he knows that these things are so, like day and night, not to be disputed. All my wilful actions and acquisitions are but roving;—the most trivial reverie, the faintest native emotion, are domestic and divine. Thoughtless people contradict as readily the statement of perceptions as of opinions, or rather much more readily; for they do not distinguish between perception and notion. They fancy that I choose to see this or that thing. But perception is not whimsical, but fatal. If I see a trait, my children will see it after me, and in course of time all mankind,—although it may chance that no one has seen it before me. For my perception of it is as much a fact as the sun.

The relations of the soul to the divine spirit are so pure that it is profane to seek to interpose helps. It must be that when God speaketh he should communicate, not one thing, but all things; should fill the world with his voice; should scatter forth light, nature, time, souls, from the center of the present thought; and new date and new create the whole. Whenever a mind is simple and receives a divine wisdom, then old things pass away,—means, teachers, texts, temples fall; it lives now, and absorbs past and future into the present hour. All things are made sacred by relation to it,—one thing as much as another. All things are dissolved to their center by their cause, and in the universal miracle petty and particular miracles disappear. This is and must be. If therefore a man claims to know and speak of God and carries you backward to the phraseology of some old moldered nation in another country, in another world, believe him not. Is the acorn better than the oak which is its fulness and completion? Is the parent better than the child into whom he has cast his ripened being? Whence then this worship of the past? The centuries are conspirators against the sanity and majesty of the soul. Time and space are but physiological colors which the eye maketh, but the soul is light; where it is, is day; where it was, is night; and history is an impertinence and an injury if it be any thing more than a cheerful apologue or parable of my being and becoming.

Man is timid and apologetic; he is no longer upright; he dares not say "I think," "I am," but quotes some saint or sage. He is ashamed before the blade of grass or the blowing rose. These roses under my window make no reference to former roses or to better ones; they are for what they are; they exist with God to-day. There is no time to them. There is simply the rose; it is perfect in every moment of its existence. Before a leaf-bud has burst, its whole life acts; in the full-blown flower there is no more; in the leafless root there is no less. Its nature is satisfied and it satisfies nature in all moments alike. There is no time to it. But man postpones or remembers; he does not live in the present, but with reverted eye laments the past, or, heedless of the riches that surround him, stands on tiptoe to foresee the future. He cannot be happy and strong until he too lives with nature in the present, above time.

This should be plain enough. Yet see what strong intellects dare not yet hear God himself unless he speak the phraseology of I know not what David, or Jeremiah, or Paul. We shall not always set so great a price on a few texts, on a few lives. We are like children who repeat by rote the sentences of grandames and tutors, and, as they grow older, of the men of talents and character they chance to see,—painfully recollecting the exact words they spoke; afterward, when they come into the point of view which those had who uttered these sayings, they understand them and are willing to let the words go; for at any time they can use words as good when occasion comes. So was it with us, so will it be, if we proceed. If we live truly, we shall see truly. It is as easy for the strong man to be strong, as it is for the weak to be weak. When we have new perception, we shall gladly disburden the memory of its hoarded treasures as old rubbish. When a man lives with God, his voice shall be as sweet as the murmur of the brook and the rustle of the corn.

And now at last the highest truth on this subject remains unsaid; probably cannot be said; for all that we say is the far off remembering of the intuition: That thought, by what I can now nearest approach to say it, is this: When good is near you, when you have life in yourself,—it is not by any known or appointed way; you shall not discern the foot-prints of any other; you shall not see the face of man; you shall not hear any name;—the way, the thought, the good, shall be wholly strange and new. It shall exclude all other being. You take the way from man, not to man. All persons that ever existed are its fugitive ministers. There shall be no fear in it. Fear and hope are alike beneath it. It asks nothing. There is somewhat low even in hope. We are then in vision. There is nothing that can be called gratitude, nor properly joy. The soul is raised over passion. It seeth identity and eternal causation. It is a perceiving that Truth and Right are. Hence it becomes a Tranquillity out of the knowing that all things go well. Vast spaces of nature; the Atlantic Ocean, the South Sea; vast intervals of time, years, centuries, are of no account. This which I think and feel underlay that former state of life and circumstances, as it does underlie my present and will always all circumstances, and what is called life and what is called death.

FOOTNOTES:

[Footnote 1: From Essays, First Series, 1841; the second half of the essay has here been omitted.]

EARLY EDUCATION AT HERNE HILL[2]

JOHN RUSKIN

When I was about four years old my father found himself able to buy the lease of a house on Herne Hill, a rustic eminence four miles south of the "Standard in Cornhill"; of which the leafy seclusion remains, in all essential points of character, unchanged to this day: certain Gothic splendours, lately indulged in by our wealthier neighbours, being the only serious innovations; and these are so graciously concealed by the fine trees of their grounds, that the passing viator remains unappalled by them; and I can still walk up and down the piece of road between the Fox tavern and the Herne Hill station, imagining myself four years old.

Our house was the northernmost of a group which stand accurately on the top or dome of the hill, where the ground is for a small space level, as the snows are, (I understand), on the dome of Mont Blanc; presently falling, however, in what may be, in the London clay formation, considered a precipitous slope, to our valley of Chamouni (or of Dulwich) on the east; and with a softer descent into Cold Harbor lane on the west: on the south, no less beautifully declining to the dale of the Effra, (doubtless shortened from Effrena, signifying the "Unbridled" river; recently, I regret to say, bricked over for the convenience of Mr. Biffin, chemist, and others); while on the north, prolonged indeed with slight depression some half mile or so, and receiving, in the parish of Lambeth, the chivalric title of "Champion Hill," it plunges down at last to efface itself in the plains of Peckham, and the rural barbarism of Goose Green.

The group, of which our house was the quarter, consisted of two precisely similar partner-couples of houses, gardens and all to match; still the two highest blocks of buildings seen from Norwood on the crest of the ridge; so that the house itself, three-storied, with garrets above, commanded, in those comparatively smokeless days, a very notable view from its garret windows, of the Norwood hills on one side, and the winter sunrise over them; and of the valley of the Thames on the other, with Windsor telescopically clear in the distance, and Harrow, conspicuous always in fine weather to open vision against the summer sunset. It had front and back garden in sufficient proportion to its size; the front, richly set with old evergreens, and well-grown lilac and laburnum; the back, seventy yards long by twenty wide, renowned over all the hill for its pears and apples, which had been chosen with extreme care by our predecessor, (shame on me to forget the name of a man to whom I owe so much!)—and possessing also a strong old mulberry tree, a tall white-heart cherry tree, a black Kentish one, and an almost unbroken hedge, all round, of alternate gooseberry and currant bush; decked, in due season, (for the ground was wholly beneficent), with magical splendour of abundant fruit: fresh green, soft amber, and rough-bristled crimson bending the spinous branches; clustered pearl and pendent ruby joyfully discoverable under the large leaves that looked like vine.

The differences of primal importance which I observed between the nature of this garden, and that of Eden, as I had imagined it, were, that, in this one, *all* the fruit was forbidden; and there were no companionable beasts: in other respects the little domain answered every purpose of paradise to me; and the climate, in that cycle of our years, allowed me to pass most of my life in it. My mother never gave me more to learn than she knew I could easily get learnt, if I set myself honestly to work, by twelve o'clock. She never allowed anything to disturb me when my task was set; if it was not said rightly by twelve o'clock, I was kept in till I knew it, and in general, even when Latin Grammar came to supplement the Psalms, I was my own master for at least an hour before half-past one dinner, and for the rest of the afternoon.

My mother, herself finding her chief personal pleasure in her flowers, was often planting, or pruning beside me, at least if I chose to stay beside *her*. I never thought of doing anything behind her back which I would not have done before her face; and her presence was therefore no restraint to me; but, also, no particular pleasure, for, from having always been left so much alone, I had generally my own little affairs to see after; and, on the whole, by the time I was seven years old, was already getting too independent, mentally, even of my father and mother; and, having nobody else to be dependent upon, began to lead a very small, perky, contented, conceited, Cock-Robinson-Crusoe sort of life, in the central point which it appeared to me, (as it must naturally appear to geometrical animals), that I occupied in the universe.

This was partly the fault of my father's modesty; and partly of his pride. He had so much more confidence in my mother's judgment as to such matters than in his own, that he never ventured even to help, much less to cross her, in the conduct of my education; on the other hand, in the fixed purpose of making an ecclesiastical gentleman of me, with the superfinest of manners, and access to the highest circles of fleshly and spiritual society, the visits to Croydon, where I entirely loved my aunt, and young baker-cousins, became rarer and more rare: the society of our neighbours on the hill could not be had without breaking up our regular and sweetly selfish manner of living; and on the whole, I had nothing animate to care for, in a childish way, but myself, some nests of ants, which the gardener would never leave undisturbed for me, and a sociable bird or two; though I never had the sense or perseverance to make one really tame. But that was partly because, if ever I managed to bring one to be the least trustful of me, the cats got it.

Under these circumstances, what powers of imagination I possessed, either fastened themselves on inanimate things,—the sky, the leaves, and pebbles, observable within the walls of Eden,—or caught at any opportunity of flight into regions of romance, compatible with the objective realities of existence in the nineteenth century, within a mile and a quarter of Camberwell Green.

Herein my father, happily, though with no definite intention other than of pleasing me, when he found he could do so without infringing any of my mother's rules, became my guide. I was particularly fond of watching him shave; and was always allowed to come into his room in the morning (under the one in which I am now writing), to be the motionless witness of that operation. Over his dressing-table hung one of his own water-colour drawings, made under the teaching of the elder Nasmyth; I believe, at the High School of Edinburgh. It was done in the early manner of tinting, which, just about the time when my father was at the High School, Dr. Munro was teaching Turner; namely, in gray under-tints of Prussian blue and British ink, washed with warm colour afterwards on the lights. It represented Conway Castle, with its Frith, and, in the foreground, a cottage, a fisherman, and a boat at the water's edge.

When my father had finished shaving, he always told me a story about this picture. The custom began without any initial purpose of his, in consequence of my troublesome curiosity whether the fisherman lived in the cottage, and where he was going to in the boat. It being settled, for peace' sake, that he *did* live in the cottage, and was going in the boat to fish near the castle, the plot of the drama afterwards gradually thickened; and became, I believe, involved with that of the tragedy of Douglas, and of the Castle Specter, in both of which pieces my father had performed in private theatricals, before my mother, and a select Edinburgh audience, when he was a boy of sixteen, and she, at grave twenty, a model housekeeper, and very scornful and religiously suspicious of theatricals. But she was never weary of telling me, in later years, how beautiful my father looked in his Highland dress, with the high black feathers.

In the afternoons, when my father returned (always punctually) from his business, he dined, at half-past four, in the front parlour, my mother sitting beside him to hear the events of the day, and give counsel and encouragement with respect to the same;—chiefly the last, for my father was apt to be vexed if orders for sherry fell the least short of their due standard, even for a day or two. I was never present at this time, however, and only avouch what I relate by hearsay and probable conjecture; for between four and six it would have been a grave misdemeanour in me if I so much as approached the parlour door. After that, in summer time, we were all in the garden as long as the day lasted; tea under the white-heart cherry tree; or in winter and rough weather, at six o'clock in the drawing-room,—I having my cup of milk, and slice of bread-and-butter, in a little recess, with a table in front of it, wholly sacred to me; and in which I remained in the evenings as an Idol in a niche, while my mother knitted, and my father read to her,—and to me, so far as I chose to listen.

The series of the Waverley novels, then drawing towards its close, was still the chief source of delight in all households caring for literature; and I can no more recollect the time when I did not know them than when I did not know the Bible; but I have still a vivid remembrance of my father's intense expression of sorrow mixed with scorn, as he threw down Count

Robert of Paris, after reading three or four pages; and knew that the life of Scott was ended: the scorn being a very complex and bitter feeling in him, —partly, indeed, of the book itself, but chiefly of the wretches who were tormenting and selling the wrecked intellect, and not a little, deep down, of the subtle dishonesty which had essentially caused the ruin. My father never could forgive Scott his concealment of the Ballantyne partnership.

Such being the salutary pleasures of Herne Hill, I have next with deeper gratitude to chronicle what I owe to my mother for the resolutely consistent lessons which so exercised me in the Scriptures as to make every word of them familiar to my ear in habitual music,—yet in that familiarity reverenced, as transcending all thought, and ordaining all conduct.

This she effected, not by her own sayings or personal authority; but simply by compelling me to read the book thoroughly, for myself. As soon as I was able to read with fluency, she began a course of Bible work with me, which never ceased till I went to Oxford. She read alternate verses with me, watching, at first, every intonation of my voice, and correcting the false ones, till she made me understand the verse, if within my reach, rightly, and energetically. It might be beyond me altogether; that she did not care about; but she made sure that as soon as I got hold of it at all, I should get hold of it by the right end.

In this way she began with the first verse of Genesis, and went straight through, to the last verse of the Apocalypse; hard names, numbers, Levitical law, and all; and began again at Genesis the next day. If a name was hard, the better the exercise in pronunciation,—if the chapter was tiresome, the better lesson in patience,—if loathsome, the better lesson in faith that there was some use in its being so outspoken. After our chapters, (from two to three a day, according to their length, the first thing after breakfast, and no interruption from servants allowed,—none from visitors, who either joined in the reading or had to stay upstairs,—and none from any visitings or excursions, except real travelling), I had to learn a few verses by heart, or repeat, to make sure I had not lost, something of what was already known; and, with the chapters thus gradually possessed from the first word to the last, I had to learn the whole body of the fine old Scottish paraphrases, which are good, melodious, and forceful verse; and to which, together with the Bible itself, I owe the first cultivation of my ear in sound.

It is strange that of all the pieces of the Bible which my mother thus taught me, that which cost me most to learn, and which was, to my child's mind, chiefly repulsive—the 119th Psalm—has now become of all the most precious to me, in its overflowing and glorious passion of love for the Law of God, in opposition to the abuse of it by modern preachers of what they imagine to be His gospel.

But it is only by deliberate effort that I recall the long morning hours of toil, as regular as sunrise,—toil on both sides equal,—by which, year after year, my mother forced me to learn these paraphrases, and chapters, (the eighth of 1st Kings being one—try it, good reader, in a leisure hour!) allowing not so much as a syllable to be missed or misplaced; while every sentence was required to be said over and over again till she was satisfied with the accent of it. I recollect a struggle between us of about three weeks, concerning the accent of the "of" in the lines

"Shall any following spring revive
The ashes of the urn?"—

I insisting, partly in childish obstinacy, and partly in true instinct for rhythm, (being wholly careless on the subject both of urns and their contents), on reciting it with an accented *of*. It was not, I say, till after three weeks' labor, that my mother got the accent lightened on the "of" and laid on the "ashes," to her mind. But had it taken three years she would have done it, having once undertaken to do it. And, assuredly, had she not done it,—well, there's no knowing what would have happened; but I'm very thankful she *did*.

I have just opened my oldest (in use) Bible,—a small, closely, and very neatly printed volume it is, printed in Edinburgh by Sir D. Hunter Blair and J. Bruce, Printers, to the King's Most Excellent Majesty, in 1816. Yellow, now, with age, and flexible, but not unclean, with much use, except that the lower corners of the pages at 8th of 1st Kings, and 32d Deuteronomy, are worn somewhat thin and dark, the learning of these two chapters having cost me much pains. My mother's list of the chapters with which, thus learned, she established my soul in life, has just fallen out of it. I will take what indulgence the incurious reader can give me, for printing the list thus accidentally occurrent:

Exodus, chapters 15th and 20th. 2 Samuel, " 1st, from 17th verse to end. 1 Kings, " 8th. Psalms, " 23d, 32d, 90th, 91st, 103d, 112th, 119th, 139th. Proverbs, " 2d, 3d, 8th, 12th. Isaiah, " 58th. Matthew, " 5th, 6th, 7th. Acts, " 26th. 1 Corinthians, " 13th, 15th. James, " 4th. Revelation, " 5th, 6th.

And, truly, though I have picked up the elements of a little further knowledge—in mathematics, meteorology, and the like, in after life,—and owe not a little to the teaching of many people, this maternal installation of my mind in that property of chapters, I count very confidently the most precious, and, on the whole, the one *essential* part of all my education.

And it is perhaps already time to mark what advantage and mischief, by the chances of life up to seven years old, had been irrevocably determined for me.

I will first count my blessings (as a not unwise friend once recommended me to do, continually; whereas I have a bad trick of always numbering the thorns in my fingers and not the bones in them).

And for best and truest beginning of all blessings, I had been taught the perfect meaning of Peace, in thought, act, and word.

I never had heard my father's or mother's voice once raised in any question with each other; nor seen an angry, or even slightly hurt or offended, glance in the eyes of either. I had never heard a servant scolded; nor even suddenly, passionately, or in any severe manner, blamed. I had never seen a moment's trouble or disorder in any household matter; nor anything whatever either done in a hurry, or undone in due time. I had no conception of such a feeling as anxiety; my father's occasional vexation in the afternoons, when he had only got an order for twelve butts after expecting one for fifteen, as I have just stated, was never manifested to *me*; and itself related only to the question whether his name would be a step higher or lower in the year's list of sherry exporters; for he never spent more than half his income, and therefore found himself little incommoded by occasional variations in the total of it. I had never done any wrong that I knew of—beyond occasionally delaying the commitment to heart of some improving sentence, that I might watch a wasp on the window pane, or a bird in the cherry tree; and I had never seen any grief.

Next to this quite priceless gift of Peace, I had received the perfect understanding of the natures of Obedience and Faith. I obeyed word, or lifted finger, of father or mother, simply as a ship her helm; not only without idea of resistance, but receiving the direction as a part of my own life and force, a helpful law, as necessary to me in every moral action as the law of gravity in leaping. And my practice in Faith was soon complete: nothing ever threatened me that was not inflicted, and nothing ever told me that was not true.

Peace, obedience, faith; these three for chief good; next to these, the habit of fixed attention with both eyes and mind—on which I will not further enlarge at this moment, this being the main practical faculty of my life, causing Mazzini to say of me, in conversation authentically reported, a year or two before his death, that I had "the most analytic mind in Europe." An opinion in which, so far as I am acquainted with Europe, I am myself entirely disposed to concur.

Lastly, an extreme perfection in palate and all other bodily senses, given by the utter prohibition of cake, wine, comfits, or, except in carefulest restriction, fruit; and by fine preparation of what food was given me. Such I esteem the main blessings of my childhood;—next, let me count the equally dominant calamities.

First, that I had nothing to love.

My parents were—in a sort—visible powers of nature to me, no more loved than the sun and the moon: only I should have been annoyed and puzzled if either of them had gone out; (how much, now, when both are darkened!)—still less did I love God; not that I had any quarrel with Him, or fear of Him; but simply found what people told me was His service, disagreeable; and what people told me was His book, not entertaining. I had no companions to quarrel with, neither; nobody to assist, and nobody to thank. Not a servant was ever allowed to do anything for me, but what it was their duty to do; and why should I have been grateful to the cook for cooking, or the gardener for gardening,—when the one dared not give me a baked potato without asking leave, and the other would not let my ants' nests alone, because they made the walks untidy? The evil consequence of all this was not, however, what might perhaps have been expected, that I grew up selfish or unaffectionate; but that, when affection did come, it came with violence utterly rampant and unmanageable, at least by me, who never before had anything to manage.

For (second of chief calamities) I had nothing to endure. Danger or pain of any kind I knew not: my strength was never exercised, my patience never tried, and my courage never fortified. Not that I was ever afraid of anything, —either ghosts, thunder, or beasts; and one of the nearest approaches to insubordination which I was ever tempted into as a child, was in passionate effort to get leave to play with the lion's cubs in Wombwell's menagerie.

Thirdly, I was taught no precision nor etiquette of manners; it was enough if, in the little society we saw, I remained unobtrusive, and replied to a question without shyness: but the shyness came later, and increased as I grew conscious of the rudeness arising from the want of social discipline, and found it impossible to acquire, in advanced life, dexterity in any bodily exercise, skill in any pleasing accomplishment, or ease and tact in ordinary behaviour.

Lastly, and chief of evils. My judgment of right and wrong, and powers of independent action, were left entirely undeveloped; because the bridle and blinkers were never taken off me. Children should have their times of being off duty, like soldiers; and when once the obedience, if required, is certain, the little creature should be very early put for periods of practice in complete command of itself; set on the barebacked horse of its own will, and left to break it by its own strength. But the ceaseless authority exercised over my youth left me, when cast out at last into the world, unable for some time to do more than drift with its vortices.

My present verdict, therefore, on the general tenor of my education at that time, must be, that it was at once too formal and too luxurious; leaving my character, at the most important moment for its construction, cramped indeed, but not disciplined; and only by protection innocent, instead of by practice virtuous.

FOOTNOTES:

[Footnote 2: From "Praeterita," *1885, Vol. I, Chapter II* .]

A CRISIS IN MY MENTAL HISTORY[3]

JOHN STUART MILL

From the winter of 1821, when I first read Bentham, and especially from the commencement of the Westminster Review, I had what might truly be called an object in life; to be a reformer of the world. My conception of my own happiness was entirely identified with this object. The personal sympathies I wished for were those of fellow labourers in this enterprise. I endeavoured to pick up as many flowers as I could by the way; but as a serious and permanent personal satisfaction to rest upon, my whole reliance was placed on this; and I was accustomed to felicitate myself on the certainty of a happy life which I enjoyed, through placing my happiness in something durable and distant, in which some progress might be always making, while it could never be exhausted by complete attainment. This did very well for several years, during which the general improvement going on in the world and the idea of myself as engaged with others in struggling to promote it, seemed enough to fill up an interesting and animated existence. But the time came when I awakened from this as from a dream. It was in the autumn of 1826. I was in a dull state of nerves, such as everybody is occasionally liable to; unsusceptible to enjoyment or pleasurable excitement; one of those moods when what is pleasure at other times, becomes insipid or indifferent; the state, I should think, in which converts to Methodism usually are, when smitten by their first "conviction of sin." In this frame of mind it occurred to me to put the question directly to myself: "Suppose that all your objects in life were realised; that all the changes in institutions and opinions which you are looking forward to, could be completely effected at this very instant: would this be a great joy and happiness to you?" And an irrepressible self-consciousness distinctly answered, "No!" At this my heart sank within me: the whole foundation on which my life was constructed fell down. All my happiness was to have been found in the continual pursuit of this end. The end had ceased to charm, and how could there ever again be any interest in the means? I seemed to have nothing left to live for.

At first I hoped that the cloud would pass away of itself; but it did not. A night's sleep, the sovereign remedy for the smaller vexations of life, had no effect on it. I awoke to a renewed consciousness of the woful fact. I carried it with me into all companies, into all occupations. Hardly anything had power to cause me even a few minutes' oblivion of it. For some months the cloud seemed to grow thicker and thicker. The lines in Coleridge's "Dejection"—I was not then acquainted with them—exactly describe my case:

"A grief without a pang, void, dark and drear,
A drowsy, stifled, unimpassioned grief,
Which finds no natural outlet or relief
In word, or sigh, or tear."

In vain I sought relief from my favourite books; those memorials of past nobleness and greatness from which I had always hitherto drawn strength and animation. I read them now without feeling, or with the accustomed feeling *minus* all its charm; and I became persuaded, that my love of mankind, and of excellence for its own sake, had worn itself out. I sought no comfort by speaking to others of what I felt. If I had loved any one sufficiently to make confiding my griefs a necessity, I should not have been in the condition I was. I felt, too, that mine was not an interesting, or in any way respectable distress. There was nothing in it to attract sympathy. Advice, if I had known where to seek it, would have been most precious. The words of Macbeth to the physician often occurred to my thoughts. But there was no one on whom I could build the faintest hope of such assistance. My father, to whom it would have been natural to me to have recourse in any practical difficulties, was the last person to whom, in such a case as this, I looked for help. Everything convinced me that he had no knowledge of any such mental state as I was suffering from, and that even if he could be made to understand it, he was not the physician who could heal it. My education, which was wholly his work, had been conducted without any regard to the possibility of its ending in this result; and I saw no use in giving him the pain of thinking that his plans had failed, when the failure was probably irremediable, and, at all events, beyond the power of *his* remedies. Of other friends, I had at that time none to whom I had any hope of making my condition intelligible. It was, however, abundantly intelligible to myself; and the more I dwelt upon it, the more hopeless it appeared.

My course of study had led me to believe, that all mental and moral feelings and qualities, whether of a good or of a bad kind, were the results of association; that we love one thing, and hate another, take pleasure in one sort of action or contemplation, and pain in another sort, through the clinging of pleasurable or painful ideas to those things, from the effect of education or of experience. As a corollary from this, I had always heard it maintained by my father, and was myself convinced, that the object of education should be to form the strongest possible associations of the salutary class; associations of pleasure with all things beneficial to the great

The experiences of this period had two very marked effects on my opinions and character. In the first place, they led me to adopt a theory of life, very unlike that on which I had before acted, and having much in common with what at that time I certainly had never heard of, the anti-self-consciousness theory of Carlyle. I never, indeed, wavered in the conviction that happiness is the test of all rules of conduct, and the end of life. But I now thought that this end was only to be attained by not making it the direct end. Those only are happy (I thought) who have their minds fixed on some object other than their own happiness; on the happiness of others, on the improvement of mankind, even on some art or pursuit, followed not as a means, but as itself an ideal end. Aiming thus at something else, they find happiness by the way. The enjoyments of life (such was now my theory) are sufficient to make it a pleasant thing, when they are taken *en passant*, without being made a principal object. Once make them so, and they are immediately felt to be insufficient. They will not bear a scrutinising examination. Ask yourself whether you are happy, and you cease to be so. The only chance is to treat, not happiness, but some end external to it, as the purpose of life. Let your self-consciousness, your scrutiny, your self-interrogation, exhaust themselves on that; and if otherwise fortunately circumstanced you will inhale happiness with the air you breathe, without dwelling on it or thinking about it, without either forestalling it in imagination, or putting it to flight by fatal questioning. This theory now became the basis of my philosophy of life. And I still hold to it as the best theory for all those who have but a moderate degree of sensibility and of capacity for enjoyment, that is, for the great majority of mankind.

The other important change which my opinions at this: time underwent, was that I, for the first time, gave its proper place, among the prime necessities of human well-being, to the internal culture of the individual. I ceased to attach almost exclusive importance to the ordering of outward circumstances, and the training of the human being for speculation and for action.

I had now learnt by experience that the passive susceptibilities needed to be cultivated as well as the active capacities, and required to be nourished and enriched as well as guided. I did not, for an instant, lose sight of, or undervalue, that part of the truth which I had seen before; I never turned recreant to intellectual culture, or ceased to consider the power and practice of analysis as an essential condition both of individual and of social improvement. But I thought that it had consequences which required to be corrected, by joining other kinds of cultivation with it. The maintenance of a due balance among the faculties, now seemed to me of primary importance. The cultivation of the feelings became one of the cardinal points in my ethical and philosophical creed. And my thoughts and inclinations turned in an increasing degree towards whatever seemed capable of being instrumental to that object.

I now began to find meaning in the things which I had read or heard about the importance of poetry and art as instruments of human culture. But it was some time longer before I began to know this by personal experience. The only one of the imaginative arts in which I had from childhood taken great pleasure, was music; the best effect of which (and in this it surpasses perhaps every other art) consists in exciting enthusiasm; in winding up to a high pitch those feelings of an elevated kind which are already in the character, but to which this excitement gives a glow and a fervour, which, though transitory at its utmost height, is precious for sustaining them at other times. This effect of music I had often experienced; but like all my pleasurable susceptibilities it was suspended during the gloomy period. I had sought relief again and again from this quarter, but found none. After the tide had turned, and I was in process of recovery, I had been helped forward by music, but in a much less elevated manner. I at this time first became acquainted with Weber's Oberon, and the extreme pleasure which I drew from its delicious melodies did me good, by showing me a source of pleasure to which I was as susceptible as ever. The good, however, was much impaired by the thought, that the pleasure of music (as is quite true of such pleasure as this was, that of mere tune) fades with familiarity, and requires either to be revived by intermittence, or fed by continual novelty. And it is very characteristic both of my then state, and of the general tone of my mind at this period of my life, that I was seriously tormented by the thought of the exhaustibility of musical combinations. The octave consists only of five tones and two semi-tones, which can be put together in only a limited number of ways, of which but a small proportion are beautiful: most of these, it seemed to me, must have been already discovered, and there could not be room for a long succession of Mozarts and Webers, to strike out, as these had done, entirely new and surpassingly rich veins of musical beauty. This source of anxiety may, perhaps, be thought to resemble that of the philosophers of Laputa, who feared lest the sun should be burnt out. It was, however, connected with the best feature in my character, and the only good point to be found in my very unromantic and in no way honourable distress. For though my dejection, honestly looked at, could not be called other than egotistical, produced by the ruin, as I thought, of my fabric of happiness, yet the destiny of mankind in general was ever in my thoughts, and could not be separated from my own. I felt that the flaw in my life, must be a flaw in life itself; that the question was, whether, if the reformers of society and government could succeed in their objects, and every person in the community were free and in a state of physical comfort, the pleasures of life, being no longer kept up by struggle and privation, would cease to be pleasures. And I felt that unless I could see my way to some better hope than this for human happiness in general my dejection must continue; but that if I could see such an outlet, I should then look on the world with pleasure; content as far as I was myself concerned, with any fair share of the general lot.

This state of my thoughts and feelings made the fact of my reading Wordsworth for the first time (in the autumn of 1828), an important event in my life. I took up the collection of his poems from curiosity, with no expectation of mental relief from it, though I had before resorted to poetry with that hope. In the worst period of my depression, I had read through the whole of Byron (then new to me), to try whether a poet, whose peculiar department was supposed to be that of the intenser feelings, could rouse any feeling in me. As might be expected, I got no good from this reading, but the reverse. The poet's state of mind was too like my own. His was the lament of a man who had worn out all pleasures, and who seemed to think that life, to all who possess the good things of it, must necessarily be the vapid, uninteresting thing which I found it. His Harold and Manfred had the same burden on them which I had; and I was not in a frame of mind to desire any comfort from the vehement sensual passion of his Giaours, or the sullenness of his Laras. But while Byron was exactly what did not suit my condition, Wordsworth was exactly what did. I had looked into the Excursion two or three years before, and found little in it; and I should probably have found as little, had I read it at this time. But the miscellaneous poems, in the two-volume edition of 1815 (to which little of value was added in the latter part of the author's life), proved to be the precise thing for my mental wants at that particular juncture.

In the first place, these poems addressed themselves powerfully to one of the strongest of my pleasurable susceptibilities, the love of rural objects and natural scenery; to which I had been indebted not only for much of the pleasure of my life, but quite recently for relief from one of my longest relapses into depression. In this power of rural beauty over me, there was a foundation laid for taking pleasure in Wordsworth's poetry; the more so, as his scenery lies mostly among mountains, which, owing to my early Pyrenean excursion, were my ideal of natural beauty. But Wordsworth would never have had any great effect on me, if he had merely placed before me beautiful pictures of natural scenery. Scott does this still better than Wordsworth, and a very second-rate landscape does it more effectually than any poet. What made Wordsworth's poems a medicine for my state of mind, was that they expressed, not mere outward beauty, but states of feeling, and of thought coloured by feeling, under the excitement of beauty. They seemed to be the very culture of the feelings which I was in quest of. In them I seemed to draw from a source of inward joy, of sympathetic and imaginative pleasures, which could be shared in by all human beings; which had no connection with struggle or imperfection, but would be made richer by every improvement in the physical or social condition of mankind. From them I seemed to learn what would be the perennial sources of happiness, when all the greater evils of life shall have been removed. And I felt myself at once better and happier as I came under their influence. There have certainly been, even in our own age, greater poets than Wordsworth; but poetry of deeper and loftier feeling could not have done for me at that time what his did. I needed to be made to feel that there was real, permanent happiness in tranquil contemplation. Wordsworth taught me this, not only without turning away from, but with a greatly increased interest in the common feelings and common destiny of human beings. And the delight which these poems gave me, proved that with culture of this sort, there was nothing to dread from the most confirmed habit of analysis. At the conclusion of the Poems came the famous Ode, falsely called Platonic, "Intimations of Immortality:" in which, along with more than his usual sweetness of melody and rhythm, and along with the two passages of grand imagery but bad philosophy so often quoted, I found that he too had had similar experience to mine; that he also had felt that the first freshness of youthful enjoyment of life was not lasting; but that he had sought for compensation, and found it, in the way in which he was now teaching me to find it. The result was that I gradually, but completely, emerged from my habitual depression, and was never again subject to it. I long continued to value Wordsworth less according to his intrinsic merits, than by the measure of what he had done for me. Compared with the greatest poets, he may be said to be the poet of unpoetical natures, possessed of quiet and contemplative tastes. But unpoetical natures are precisely those which require poetic cultivation. This cultivation Wordsworth is much more fitted to give, than poets who are intrinsically far more poets than he.

FOOTNOTES:

[Footnote 3: From Chapter V of the Autobiography, 1874.]

OLD CHINA[4]

CHARLES LAMB

I have an almost feminine partiality for old china. When I go to see any great house, I inquire for the china-closet, and next for the picture-gallery. I cannot defend the order of preference, but by saying that we have all some taste or other, of too ancient a date to admit of our remembering distinctly that it was an acquired one. I can call to mind the first play, and the first exhibition, that I was taken to; but I am not conscious of a time when china jars and saucers were introduced into my imagination.

I had no repugnance then—why should I now have?—to those little, lawless, azure-tinctured grotesques, that, under the notion of men and women, float about, uncircumscribed by any element in that world before perspective—a china tea-cup.

I like to see my old friends, whom distance cannot diminish, figuring up in the air (so they appear to our optics), yet on *terra firma* still—for so we must in courtesy interpret that speck of deeper blue, which the decorous artist, to prevent absurdity, had made to spring up beneath their sandals.

I love the men with women's faces, and women, if possible, with still more womanish expressions.

Here is a young and courtly Mandarin, handing tea to a lady from a salver—two miles off. See how distance seems to set off respect! And here the same lady, or another—for likeness is identity on tea-cups—is stepping into a little fairy boat, moored on the hither side of this calm garden river, with a dainty mincing foot, which in a right angle of incidence (as angles go in our world) must infallibly land her in the midst of a flowery mead—a furlong off on the other side of the same strange stream!

Further on—if far or near can be predicated of their world—see horses, trees, pagodas, dancing the hays.[5]

Here—a cow and rabbit couchant, and coextensive—so objects show, seen through the lucid atmosphere of fine Cathay.

I was pointing out to my cousin last evening, over our Hyson (which we are old-fashioned enough to drink unmixed still of an afternoon), some of these *speciosa miracula*[6] upon a set of extraordinary old blue china (a recent purchase) which we were now for the first time using; and could not help remarking, how favourable circumstances had been to us of late years, that we could afford to please the eye sometimes with trifles of this sort—when a passing sentiment seemed to overshade the brows of my companion. I am quick at detecting these summer clouds in Bridget.

"I wish the good old times would come again," she said, "when we were not quite so rich. I do not mean that I want to be poor; but there was a middle state,"—so she was pleased to ramble on,—"in which I am sure we were a great deal happier. A purchase is but a purchase, now that you have money enough and to spare. Formerly it used to be a triumph. When we coveted a cheap luxury (and, oh! how much ado I had to get you to consent in those times!) we were used to have a debate two or three days before, and to weigh the *for* and *against*, and think what we might spare it out of, and what saving we could hit upon, that should be an equivalent. A thing was worth buying then, when we felt the money that we paid for it.

"Do you remember the brown suit, which you made to hang upon you, till your friends cried shame upon you, it grew so threadbare—and all because of that folio *Beaumont and Fletcher,* which you dragged home late at night from Barker's in Covent-garden? Do you remember how we eyed it for weeks before we could make up our minds to the purchase, and had not come to a determination till it was near ten o'clock of the Saturday night, when you set off from Islington, fearing you should be too late—and when the old bookseller with some grumbling opened his shop, and by the twinkling taper (for he was setting bed-ward) lighted out the relic from his dusty treasures—and when you lugged it home, wishing it were twice as cumbersome—and when you presented it to me—and when we were exploring the perfectness of it (*collating* you called it)—and while I was repairing some of the loose leaves with paste, which your impatience would not suffer to be left till daybreak—was there no pleasure in being a poor man? or can those neat black clothes which you wear now, and are so careful to keep brushed, since we have become rich and finical, give you half the honest vanity with which you flaunted it about in that overworn suit—your old corbeau—for four or five weeks longer than you should have done, to pacify your conscience for the mighty sum of fifteen—or sixteen shillings was it?—a great affair we thought it then—which you had lavished on the old folio. Now you can afford to buy any book that pleases you, but I do not see that you ever bring me home any nice old purchases now.

"When you came home with twenty apologies for laying out a less number of shillings upon that print after Lionardo which we christened the 'Lady Blanch'; when you looked at the purchase, and thought of the money—and thought of the money, and looked again at the picture—was there no pleasure in being a poor man? Now, you have nothing to do but to walk into Colnaghi's, and buy a wilderness of Lionardos. Yet do you?

"Then, do you remember our pleasant walks to Enfield, and Potter's bar, and Waltham, when we had a holiday—holidays and all other fun are gone now we are rich—and the little handbasket in which I used to deposit our day's fare of savory cold lamb and salad—and how you would pry about at noon-tide for some decent house, where we might go in and produce our store—only paying for the ale that you must call for—and speculate upon the looks of the landlady, and whether she was likely to allow us a tablecloth—and wish for such another honest hostess as Izaak Walton has described many a one on the pleasant banks of the Lea, when he went a fishing—and sometimes they would prove obliging enough, and sometimes they would look grudgingly upon us—but we had cheerful looks still for one another, and would eat our plain food savorily, scarcely grudging Piscator[7] his Trout Hall? Now, when we go out a day's pleasuring, which is seldom, moreover, we *ride* part of the way, and go into a fine inn, and order the best of dinners, never debating the expense, which, after all, never has half the relish of those chance country snaps, when we were at the mercy of uncertain usage, and a precarious welcome.

"You are too proud to see a play anywhere now but in the pit. Do you remember where it was we used to sit, when we saw the *Battle of Hexham,* and the *Surrender of Calais,* and Bannister and Mrs. Bland in the *Children in the Wood*—when we squeezed out our shilling apiece to sit three or four times in a season in the one-shilling gallery—where you felt all the time that you ought not to have brought me—and more strongly I felt obligation to you for having brought me—and the pleasure was the better for a little shame—and when the curtain drew up, what cared we for our place in the house, or what mattered it where we were sitting, when our thoughts were with Rosalind in Arden, or with Viola at the Court of Illyria? You used to say that the gallery was the best place of all for enjoying a play socially; that the relish of such exhibitions must be in proportion to the infrequency of going; that the company we met there, not being in general readers of plays, were obliged to attend the more, and did attend, to what was going on on the stage, because a word lost would have been a chasm which it was impossible for them to fill up. With such reflections we consoled our pride then, and I appeal to you whether, as a woman, I met generally with less attention and accommodation than I have done since in more expensive situations in the house? The getting in, indeed, and the crowding up those inconvenient staircases, was bad enough,—but there was still a law of civility to woman recognised to quite as great an extent as we ever found in the other passages—and how a little difficulty overcome heightened the snug seat, and the play, afterward! Now we can only pay our money, and walk in. You cannot see, you say, in the galleries now. I am sure we saw, and heard too, well enough then—but sight, and all, I think, is gone with our poverty.

"There was pleasure in eating strawberries, before they became quite common—in the first dish of peas, while they were yet dear—to have them for a nice supper, a treat. What treat can we have now? If we were to treat ourselves now—that is, to have dainties a little above our means, it would be selfish and wicked. It is the very little more that we allow ourselves beyond what the actual poor can get at, that makes what I call a treat—when two people living together, as we have done, now and then indulge themselves in a cheap luxury, which both like; while each apologises, and is willing to take both halves of the blame to his single share. I see no harm in people making much of themselves in that sense of the word. It may give them a hint how to make much of others. But now—what I mean by the word—we never *do* make much of ourselves. None but the poor can do it. I do not mean the veriest poor of all, but persons as we were, just above poverty.

"I know what you were going to say, that it is mighty pleasant at the end of the year to make all meet,—and much ado we used to have every Thirty-first Night of December to account for our exceedings—many a long face did you make over your puzzled accounts, and in contriving to make it out how we had spent so much—or that we had not spent so much—or that it was impossible we should spend so much next year—and still we found our slender capital decreasing—but then, betwixt ways, and projects, and compromises of one sort or another and talk of curtailing this charge, and doing without that for the future—and the hope that youth brings, and laughing spirits (in which you were never poor till now), we pocketed up our loss, and in conclusion, with 'lusty brimmers' (as you used to quote it out of *hearty, cheerful Mr. Cotton*[8], as you called him), we used to welcome in the 'coming guest.' Now we have no reckoning at all at the end of the old year; no flattering promises about the new year doing better for us."

Bridget is so sparing of her speech, on most occasions, that when she gets into a rhetorical vein, I am careful how I interrupt it. I could not help, however, smiling at the phantom of wealth which her dear imagination had conjured up out of a clear income of poor —— hundred pounds a year. "It is true we were happier when we were poorer, but we were also younger, my cousin. I am afraid we must put up with the excess, for if we were to shake the superflux into the sea, we should not much mend ourselves. That we had much to struggle with, as we grew up together, we have reason to be most thankful. It strengthened and knit our compact closer. We could never have been what we have been to each other, if we had always had the sufficiency which you now complain of. The resisting power, those natural dilations of the youthful spirit, which circumstances can not straiten—with us are long since passed away. Competence to age is supplementary youth, a sorry supplement indeed, but I fear the best that is to be had. We must ride where we formerly walked: live better and lie softer—and shall be wise to do so—than we had means to do in those good old days you speak of. Yet could those days return, could you and I once more walk our thirty miles a day, could Bannister and Mrs. Bland again be young, and you and I be young to see them, could the good old one shilling gallery days return—they are dreams, my cousin, now, but could you and I at this moment, instead of this quiet argument, by our well-carpeted fireside, sitting on this luxurious sofa—be once more struggling up those inconvenient staircases, pushed about and squeezed, and elbowed by the poorest rabble of poor gallery scramblers—could I once more hear those anxious shrieks of yours, and the delicious *Thank God, we are safe,* which always followed, when the topmost stair, conquered, let in the first light of the whole cheerful theatre down beneath us—I know not the fathom line that ever touched a descent so deep as I would be willing to bury more wealth in than Croesus had, or the great Jew R—— is supposed to have, to purchase it. And now do just look at that merry little Chinese waiter holding an umbrella, big enough for a bed-tester, over the head of that pretty insipid half-Madonna-ish chit of a lady in that very blue summer-house."

FOOTNOTES:

[Footnote 4: From "Last Essays of Elia," 1833.]

[Footnote 5: The hays: an old English dance.]

[Footnote 6: Speciosa miracula: beautiful marvels.]

[Footnote 7: Piscator: The Angler—the author's spokesman in Walton's "The Complete Angler."]

[Footnote 8: Charles Cotton, a humorist of the seventeenth century.]

WHAT IS EDUCATION?[9]

THOMAS HENRY HUXLEY

What is education? Above all things, what is our ideal of a thoroughly liberal education?—of that education which, if we could begin life again, we would give ourselves—of that education which, if we could mould the fates to our own will, we would give our children? Well, I know not what may be your conceptions upon this matter, but I will tell you mine, and I hope I shall find that our views are not very discrepant.

Suppose it were perfectly certain that the life and fortune of every one of us would, one day or other, depend upon his winning or losing a game of chess. Don't you think that we should all consider it to be a primary duty to learn at least the names and the moves of the pieces; to have a notion of a gambit, and a keen eye for all the means of giving and getting out of check? Do you not think that we should look with a disapprobation amounting to scorn, upon the father who allowed his son, or the state which allowed its members, to grow up without knowing a pawn from a knight?

Yet it is a very plain and elementary truth, that the life, the fortune, and the happiness of every one of us, and, more or less, of those who are connected with us, do depend upon our knowing something of the rules of a game infinitely more difficult and complicated than chess. It is a game which has been played for untold ages, every man and woman of us being one of the two players in a game of his or her own. The chess-board is the world, the pieces are the phenomena of the universe, the rules of the game are what we call the laws of Nature. The player on the other side is hidden from us. We know that his play is always fair, just and patient. But also we know, to our cost, that he never overlooks a mistake, or makes the smallest allowance for ignorance. To the man who plays well, the highest stakes are paid, with that sort of overflowing generosity with which the strong shows delight in strength. And one who plays ill is checkmated—without haste, but without remorse.

My metaphor will remind some of you of the famous picture in which Retzsch has depicted Satan playing at chess with man for his soul. Substitute for the mocking fiend in that picture a calm, strong angel who is playing for love, as we say, and would rather lose than win—and I should accept it as an image of human life.

Well, what I mean by Education is learning the rules of this mighty game. In other words, education is the instruction of the intellect in the laws of Nature, under which name I include not merely things and their forces, but men and their ways; and the fashioning of the affections and of the will into an earnest and loving desire to move in harmony with those laws. For me, education means neither more nor less than this. Anything which professes to call itself education must be tried by this standard, and if it fails to stand the test, I will not call it education, whatever may be the force of authority, or of numbers, upon the other side.

It is important to remember that, in strictness, there is no such thing as an uneducated man. Take an extreme case. Suppose that an adult man, in the full vigour of his faculties, could be suddenly placed in the world, as Adam is said to have been, and then left to do as he best might. How long would he be left uneducated? Not five minutes. Nature would begin to teach him, through the eye, the ear, the touch, the properties of objects. Pain and pleasure would be at his elbow telling him to do this and avoid that; and by slow degrees the man would receive an education which, if narrow, would be thorough, real, and adequate to his circumstances, though there would be no extras and very few accomplishments.

And if to this solitary man entered a second Adam, or, better still, an Eve, a new and greater world, that of social and moral phenomena, would be revealed. Joys and woes, compared with which all others might seem but faint shadows, would spring from the new relations. Happiness and sorrow would take the place of the coarser monitors, pleasure and pain; but conduct would still be shaped by the observation of the natural consequences of actions; or, in other words, by the laws of the nature of man.

To every one of us the world was once as fresh and new as to Adam. And then, long before we were susceptible of any other modes of instruction, Nature took us in hand, and every minute of waking life brought its educational influence, shaping our actions into rough accordance with Nature's laws, so that we might not be ended untimely by too gross disobedience. Nor should I speak of this process of education as past for any one, be he as old as he may. For every man the world is as fresh as it was at the first day, and as full of untold novelties for him who has the eyes to see them. And Nature is still continuing her patient education of us in that great university, the universe, of which we are all members—Nature having no Test-Acts.

Those who take honours in Nature's university, who learn the laws which govern men and things and obey them, are the really great and successful men in this world. The great mass of mankind are the "Poll,"[10] who pick up just enough to get through without much discredit. Those who won't learn at all are plucked; and then you can't come up again. Nature's pluck means extermination.

Thus the question of compulsory education is settled so far as Nature is concerned. Her bill on that question was framed and passed long ago. But, like all compulsory legislation, that of Nature is harsh and wasteful in its operation. Ignorance is visited as sharply as wilful disobedience—incapacity meets with the same punishment as crime. Nature's discipline is not even a word and a blow, and the blow first; but the blow without the word. It is left to you to find out why your ears are boxed.

The object of what we commonly call education—that education in which man intervenes and which I shall distinguish as artificial education—is to make good these defects in Nature's methods; to prepare the child to receive Nature's education, neither incapably nor ignorantly, nor with wilful disobedience; and to understand the preliminary symptoms of her pleasure, without waiting for the box on the ear. In short, all artificial education ought to be an anticipation of natural education. And a liberal education is an artificial education which has not only prepared a man to escape the great evils of disobedience to natural laws, but has trained him to appreciate and to seize upon the rewards, which Nature scatters with as free a hand as her penalties.

That man, I think, has had a liberal education who has been so trained in youth that his body is the ready servant of his will, and does with ease and pleasure all the work that, as a mechanism, it is capable of; whose intellect is a clear, cold, logic engine, with all its parts of equal strength, and in smooth working order; ready, like a steam engine, to be turned to any kind of work, and spin the gossamers as well as forge the anchors of the mind; whose mind is stored with a knowledge of the great and fundamental truths of Nature and of the laws of her operations; one who, no stunted ascetic, is full of life and fire, but whose passions are trained to come to heel by a vigorous will, the servant of a tender conscience; who has learned to love all beauty, whether of Nature or of art, to hate all vileness, and to respect others as himself.

Such an one and no other, I conceive, has had a liberal education; for he is, as completely as a man can be, in harmony with Nature. He will make the best of her, and she of him. They will get on together rarely; she as his ever beneficent mother; he as her mouthpiece, her conscious self, her minister and interpreter.

FOOTNOTES:

[Footnote 9: From "A Liberal Education; and Where to Find It," 1868.]

[Footnote 10: Poll (a slang term used at Cambridge University): those who take a degree without honours.]

KNOWLEDGE VIEWED IN RELATION TO LEARNING[11]

JOHN HENRY NEWMAN

It were well if the English, like the Greek language, possessed some definite word to express, simply and generally, intellectual proficiency or perfection, such as "health," as used with reference to the animal frame, and "virtue," with reference to our moral nature. I am not able to find such a term;—talent, ability, genius, belong distinctly to the raw material, which is the subject-matter, not to that excellence which is the result of exercise and training. When we turn, indeed, to the particular kinds of intellectual perfection, words are forthcoming for our purpose, as, for instance, judgment, taste, and skill; yet even these belong, for the most part, to powers or habits bearing upon practice or upon art, and not to any perfect condition of the intellect, considered in itself. Wisdom, again, is certainly a more comprehensive word than any other, but it has a direct relation to conduct, and to human life. Knowledge, indeed, and science express purely intellectual ideas but still not a state or quality of the intellect; for knowledge, in its ordinary sense, is but one of its circumstances, denoting a possession or a habit; and science has been appropriated to the subject-matter of the intellect, instead of belonging in English, as it ought to do, to the intellect itself. The consequence is that, on an occasion like this, many words are necessary, in order, first, to bring out and convey what surely is no difficult idea in itself,—that of the cultivation of the intellect as an end; next, in order to recommend what surely is no unreasonable object; and lastly, to describe and make the mind realise the particular perfection in which that object consists. Every one knows practically what are the constituents of health or of virtue; and every one recognises health and virtue as ends to be pursued; it is otherwise with intellectual excellence, and this must be my excuse, if I seem to anyone to be bestowing a good deal of labour on a preliminary matter.

In default of a recognised term, I have called the perfection or virtue of the intellect by the name of philosophy, philosophical knowledge, enlargement of mind, or illumination, terms which are not uncommonly given to it by writers of this day: but, whatever name we bestow on it, it is, I believe, as a matter of history, the business of a university to make this intellectual culture its direct scope, or to employ itself in the education of the intellect,—just as the work of a hospital lies in healing the sick or wounded, of a riding or fencing school, or of a gymnasium, in exercising the limbs, of an almshouse, in aiding and solacing the old, of an orphanage, in protecting innocence, of a penitentiary, in restoring the guilty. I say, a university, taken in its bare idea, and before we view it as an instrument of the church, has this object and this mission; it contemplates neither moral impression nor mechanical production; it professes to exercise the mind neither in art nor in duty; its function is intellectual culture; here it may leave its scholars, and it has done its work when it has done as much as this. It educates the intellect to reason well in all matters, to reach out towards truth, and to grasp it.

This, I said in my foregoing discourse, was the object of a university, viewed in itself, and apart from the Catholic Church, or from the state, or from any other power which may use it; and I illustrated this in various ways. I said that the intellect must have an excellence of its own, for there was nothing which had not its specific good; that the word "educate" would not be used of intellectual culture, as it is used, had not the intellect had an end of its own; that, had it not such an end, there would be no meaning in calling certain intellectual exercises "liberal," in contrast with "useful," as is commonly done; that the very notion of a philosophical temper implied it, for it threw us back upon research and system as ends in themselves, distinct from effects and works of any kind; that a philosophical scheme of knowledge, or system of sciences, could not, from the nature of the case, issue in any one definite art or pursuit, as its end; and that, on the other hand, the discovery and contemplation of truth, to which research and systematising led, were surely sufficient ends, though nothing beyond them were added, and that they had ever been accounted sufficient by mankind.

Here then I take up the subject; and having determined that the cultivation of the intellect is an end distinct and sufficient in itself, and that, so far as words go, it is an enlargement or illumination. I proceed to inquire what this mental breadth, or power, or light, or philosophy consists in. A hospital heals a broken limb or cures a fever: what does an institution effect, which professes the health, not of the body, not of the soul, but of the intellect? What is this good, which in former times, as well as our own, has been found worth the notice, the appropriation of the Catholic Church?

I have then to investigate, in the discourses which follow, those qualities and characteristics of the intellect in which its cultivation issues or rather consists; and, with a view of assisting myself in this undertaking, I shall recur to certain questions which have already been touched upon. These questions are three: viz. the relation of intellectual culture, first, to *mere* knowledge; secondly, to *professional* knowledge; and thirdly, to *religious* knowledge. In other words, are *acquirements* and *attainments* the scope of a university education? or *expertness in particular arts* and *pursuits*? or *moral and religious proficiency*? or something besides these three? These questions I shall examine in succession, with the purpose I have mentioned; and I hope to be excused, if, in this anxious undertaking, I am led to repeat what, either in these discourses or elsewhere, I have already put upon paper. And first, of *mere knowledge,* or learning, and its connection with intellectual illumination or philosophy.

I suppose the *prima-facie*[12] view which the public at large would take of a university, considering it as a place of education, is nothing more or less than a place for acquiring a great deal of knowledge on a great many subjects. Memory is one of the first developed of the mental faculties; a boy's business when he goes to school is to learn, that is, to store up things in his memory. For some years his intellect is little more than an instrument for taking in facts, or a receptacle for storing them; he welcomes them as fast as they come to him; he lives on what is without; he has his eyes ever about him; he has a lively susceptibility of impressions; he imbibes information of every kind; and little does he make his own in a true sense of the word, living rather upon his neighbours all around him. He has opinions, religious, political and literary, and, for a boy, is very positive in them and sure about them; but he gets them from his schoolfellows, or his masters, or his parents, as the case may be. Such as he is in his other relations, such also is he in his school exercises; his mind is observant, sharp, ready, retentive; he is almost passive in the acquisition of knowledge. I say this in no disparagement of the idea of a clever boy. Geography, chronology, history, language, natural history, he heaps up the matter of these studies as treasures for a future day. It is the seven years of plenty with him: he gathers in by handfuls, like the Egyptians, without counting; and though, as time goes on, there is exercise for his argumentative powers in the elements of mathematics, and for his taste in the poets and orators, still, while at school, or at least, till quite the last years of his time, he acquires, and little more; and when he is leaving for the university, he is mainly the creature of foreign influences and circumstances, and made up of accidents, homogeneous or not, as the case may be. Moreover, the moral habits, which are a boy's praise, encourage and assist this result; that is, diligence, assiduity, regularity, despatch, persevering application; for these are the direct conditions of acquisition, and naturally lead to it. Acquirements, again, are emphatically producible, and at a moment; they are a something to show, both for master and scholar; an audience, even though ignorant themselves of the subjects of an examination, can comprehend when questions are answered and when they are not. Here again is a reason why mental culture is in the minds of men identified with the acquisition of knowledge.

The same notion possesses the public mind, when it passes on from the thought of a school to that of a university: and with the best of reasons so far as this, that there is no true culture without acquirements, and that philosophy presupposes knowledge. It requires a great deal of reading, or a wide range of information, to warrant us in putting forth our opinions on any serious subject; and without such learning the most original mind may be able indeed to dazzle, to amuse, to refute, to perplex, but not to come to any useful result or any trustworthy conclusion. There are indeed persons who profess a different view of the matter, and even act upon it. Every now and then you will find a person of vigorous or fertile mind, who relies upon his own resources, despises all former authors, and gives the world, with the utmost fearlessness, his views upon religion, or history, or any other popular subject. And his works may sell for a while; he may get a name in his day; but this will be all. His readers are sure to find on the long run that his doctrines are mere theories, and not the expression of facts, that they are chaff instead of bread, and then his popularity drops as suddenly as it rose.

Knowledge then is the indispensable condition of expansion of mind, and the instrument of attaining to it; this cannot be denied, it is ever to be insisted on; I begin with it as a first principle; however, the very truth of it carries men too far, and confirms to them the notion that it is the whole of the matter. A narrow mind is thought to be that which contains little knowledge; and an enlarged mind, that which holds a great deal; and what seems to put the matter beyond dispute is, the fact of the great number of studies which are pursued in a university, by its very profession. Lectures are given on every kind of subject; examinations are held; prizes awarded. There are moral, metaphysical, physical professors; professors of languages, of history, of mathematics, of experimental science. Lists of questions are published, wonderful for their range and depth, variety and difficulty; treatises are written, which carry upon their very face the evidence of extensive reading or multifarious information; what then is wanting for mental culture to a person of large reading and scientific attainments? what is grasp of mind but acquirement? where shall philosophical repose be found, but in the consciousness and enjoyment of large intellectual possessions?

And yet this notion is, I conceive, a mistake, and my present business is to show that it is one, and that the end of a liberal education is not mere knowledge, or knowledge considered in its *matter*; and I shall best attain my object, by actually setting down some cases, which will be generally granted to be instances of the process of enlightenment or enlargement of mind, and others which are not, and thus, by the comparison, you will be able to judge for yourselves, gentlemen, whether knowledge, that is, acquirement, is after all the real principle of the enlargement or whether that principle is not rather something beyond it.

For instance, let a person, whose experience has hitherto been confined to the more calm and unpretending scenery of these islands, whether here or in England, go for the first time into parts where physical nature puts on her wilder and more awful forms, whether at home or abroad, as into mountainous districts; or let one, who has ever lived in a quiet village, go for the first time to a great metropolis,—then I suppose he will have a sensation which perhaps he never had before. He has a feeling not in addition or increase of former feelings, but of something different in its nature. He will perhaps be borne forward, and find for a time that he has lost his bearings. He has made a certain progress, and he has a consciousness of mental enlargement; he does not stand where he did, he has a new centre, and a range of thoughts to which he was before a stranger.

Again, the view of the heavens which the telescope opens upon us, if allowed to fill and possess the mind, may almost whirl it round and make it dizzy. It brings in a flood of ideas, and is rightly called an intellectual enlargement, whatever is meant by the term.

And so again, the sight of beasts of prey and other foreign animals, their strangeness, the originality (if I may use the term) of their forms and gestures and habits, and their variety and independence of each other, throw us out of ourselves into another creation, and as if under another Creator, if I may so express the temptation which may come on the mind. We seem to have new faculties, or a new exercise for our faculties, by this addition to our knowledge; like a prisoner, who, having been accustomed to wear manacles or fetters, suddenly finds his arms and legs free.

Hence physical science generally, in all its departments, as bringing before us the exuberant riches and resources, yet the orderly course, of the universe, elevates and excites the student, and at first, I may say, almost takes away his breath, while in time it exercises a tranquillising influence upon him.

Again the study of history is said to enlarge and enlighten the mind, and why? because, as I conceive, it gives it a power of judging of passing events and of all events, and a conscious superiority over them, which before it did not possess.

And in like manner, what is called seeing the world, entering into active life, going into society, travelling, gaining acquaintance with the various classes of the community, coming into contact with the principles and modes of thought of various parties, interests, and races, their views, aims, habits and manners, their religious creeds and forms of worship,—gaining experience how various yet how alike men are, how low-minded, how bad, how opposed, yet how confident in their opinions; all this exerts a perceptible influence upon the mind, which it is impossible to mistake, be it good or be it bad, and is popularly called its enlargement.

And then again, the first time the mind comes across the arguments and speculations of unbelievers, and feels what a novel light they cast upon what he has hitherto accounted sacred; and still more, if it gives in to them and embraces them, and throws off as so much prejudice what it has hitherto held, and, as if waking from a dream, begins to realise to its imagination that there is now no such thing as law and the transgression of law, that sin is a phantom, and punishment a bugbear, that it is free to sin, free to enjoy the world and the flesh; and still further, when it does enjoy them, and reflects that it may think and hold just what it will, that "the world is all before it where to choose," and what system to build up as its own private persuasion; when this torrent of wilful thoughts rushes over and inundates it, who will deny that the fruit of the tree of knowledge, or what the mind takes for knowledge, has made it one of the gods, with a sense of expansion and elevation,—an intoxication in reality, still, so far as the subjective state of the mind goes, an illumination? Hence the fanaticism of individuals or nations, who suddenly cast off their Maker. Their eyes are opened; and, like the judgment-stricken king in the tragedy, they see two suns, and a magic universe, out of which they look back upon their former state of faith and innocence with a sort of contempt and indignation, as if they were then but fools, and the dupes of imposture.

On the other hand, religion has its own enlargement, and an enlargement, not of tumult, but of peace. It is often remarked of uneducated persons, who have hitherto thought little of the unseen world, that, on their turning to God, looking into themselves, regulating their hearts, reforming their conduct, and meditating on death and judgment, heaven and hell, they seem to become, in point of intellect, different beings from what they were. Before, they took things as they came, and thought no more of one thing than another. But now every event has a meaning; they have their own estimate of whatever happens to them; they are mindful of times and seasons, and compare the present with the past; and the world, no longer dull, monotonous, unprofitable, and hopeless, is a various and complicated drama, with parts and an object, and an awful moral.

Now from these instances, to which many more might be added, it is plain, first, that the communication of knowledge certainly is either a condition or the means of that sense of enlargement or enlightenment, of which at this day we hear so much in certain quarters: this cannot be denied; but next, it is equally plain, that such communication is not the whole of the process. The enlargement consists, not merely in the passive reception into the mind of a number of ideas hitherto unknown to it, but in the mind's energetic and simultaneous action upon and towards and among those new ideas, which are rushing in upon it. It is the action of a formative power, reducing to order and meaning the matter of our acquirements; it is a making the objects of our knowledge subjectively our own, or, to use a familiar word, it is a digestion of what we receive, into the substance of our previous state of thought; and without this no enlargement is said to follow. There is no enlargement, unless there be a comparison of ideas one with another, as they come before the mind, and a systematising of them. We feel our minds to be growing and expanding *then,* when we not only learn, but refer what we learn to what we know already. It is not the mere addition to our knowledge that is the illumination; but the locomotion, the movement onwards, of that mental centre, to which both what we know, and what we are learning, the accumulating mass of our acquirements, gravitates. And therefore a truly great intellect, and recognised to be such by the common opinion of mankind, such as the intellect of Aristotle, or of St. Thomas, or of Newton, or of Goethe (I purposely take instances within and without the Catholic pale, when I would speak of the intellect as such), is one which takes a connected view of old and new, past and present, far and near, and which has an insight into the influence of all these one on another; without which there is no whole and no centre. It possesses the knowledge, not only of things, but also of their mutual and true relations; knowledge, not merely considered as acquirement but as philosophy.

Accordingly, when this analytical, distributive, harmonising process is away, the mind experiences no enlargement, and is not reckoned as enlightened or comprehensive, whatever it may add to its knowledge. For instance, a great memory, as I have already said, does not make a philosopher, any more than a dictionary can be called a grammar. There are men who embrace in their minds a vast multitude of ideas, but with little sensibility about their real relations towards each other. These may be antiquarians, annalists, naturalists; they may be learned in the law; they may be versed in statistics; they are most useful in their own place; I should shrink from speaking disrespectfully of them; still, there is nothing in such attainments to guarantee the absence of narrowness of mind. If they are nothing more than well-read men, or men of information, they have not what specially deserves the name of culture of mind, or fulfils the type of liberal education.

In like manner, we sometimes fall in with persons who have seen much of the world, and of the men who, in their day, have played a conspicuous part in it, but who generalise, nothing, and have no observation, in the true sense of the word. They abound in information in detail, curious and entertaining, about men and things; and, having lived under the influence of no very clear or settled principles, religious or political, they speak of every one and every thing, only as so many phenomena, which are complete in themselves, and lead to nothing, not discussing them, or teaching any truth, or instructing the hearer, but simply talking. No one would say that these persons, well informed as they are, had attained to any great culture of intellect or to philosophy.

The case is the same still more strikingly where the persons in question are beyond dispute men of inferior powers and deficient education. Perhaps they have been much in foreign countries, and they receive, in a passive, otiose, unfruitful way, the various facts which are forced upon them there. Seafaring men, for example, range from one end of the earth to the other; but the multiplicity of external objects, which they have encountered, forms no symmetrical and consistent picture upon their imagination; they see the tapestry of human life, as it were on the wrong side, and it tells no story. They sleep, and they rise up, and they find themselves, now in Europe, now in Asia; they see visions of great cities and wild regions; they are in the marts of commerce, or amid the islands of the South; they gaze on Pompey's Pillar, or on the Andes; and nothing which meets them carries them forward or backward, to any idea beyond itself. Nothing has a drift or relation; nothing has a history or a promise. Every thing stands by itself, and comes and goes in its turn, like the shifting scenes of a show, which leave the spectator where he was. Perhaps you are near such a man on a particular occasion, and expect him to be shocked or perplexed at something which occurs; but one thing is much the same to him as another, or, if he is perplexed, it is as not knowing what to say, whether it is right to admire, or to ridicule or to disapprove, while conscious that some expression of opinion is expected from him; for in fact he has no standard of judgment at all, and no landmarks to guide him to a conclusion. Such is mere acquisition, and, I repeat, no one would dream of calling it philosophy.

Instances, such as these, confirm, by the contrast, the conclusion I have already drawn from those which preceded them. That only is true enlargement of mind which is the power of viewing many things at once as one whole, of referring them severally to their true place in the universal system, of understanding their respective values, and determining their mutual dependence. Thus is that form of universal knowledge, of which I have on a former occasion spoken, set up in the individual intellect, and constitutes its perfection. Possessed of this real illumination, the mind never views any part of the extended subject-matter of knowledge without recollecting that it is but a part, or without the associations which spring from this recollection. It makes everything in some sort lead to everything else; it would communicate the image of the whole to every separate portion, till that whole becomes in imagination like a spirit, everywhere pervading and penetrating its component parts, and giving them one definite meaning. Just as our bodily organs, when mentioned, recall their function in the body, as the word "creation" suggests the Creator, and "subjects" a sovereign, so, in the mind of the philosopher as we are abstractedly conceiving of him, the elements of the physical and moral world, sciences, arts, pursuits, ranks, offices, events, opinions, individualities, are all viewed as one with correlative functions, and as gradually by successive combinations converging, one and all, to the true centre.

To have even a portion of this illuminative reason and true philosophy is the highest state to which nature can aspire, in the way of intellect; it puts the mind above the influences of chance and necessity, above anxiety, suspense, unsettlement, and superstition, which is the lot of the many. Men, whose minds are possessed with some one object, take exaggerated views of its importance, are feverish in the pursuit of it, make it the measure of things which are utterly foreign to it, and are startled and despond if it happens to fail them. They are ever in alarm or in transport. Those on the other hand who have no object or principle whatever to hold by, lose their way every step they take. They are thrown out, and do not know what to think or say, at every fresh juncture; they have no view of persons, or occurrences, or facts, which come suddenly upon them, and they hang upon the opinion of others for want of internal resources. But the intellect, which has been disciplined to the perfection of its powers, which knows, and thinks while it knows, which has learned to leaven the dense mass of facts and events with the elastic force of reason, such an intellect cannot be partial, cannot be exclusive, cannot be impetuous, cannot be at a loss, cannot but be patient, collected, and majestically calm, because it discerns the end in every beginning, the origin in every end, the law in every interruption, the limit in each delay; because it ever knows where it stands, and how its path lies from one point to another. It is the [Greek: tetragonos] [13] of the Peripatetic, and has the *nil admirari*[14] of the Stoic,—

 Felix qui potuit rerum cognoscere causas,
 Atque metus omnes, et inexorabile fatum
 Subjecit pedibus, strepitumque Acherontis avari.[15]

 There are men who, when in difficulties, originate at the moment vast ideas or dazzling projects; who, under the influence of excitement, are able to cast a light, almost as if from inspiration, on a subject or course of action which comes before them; who have a sudden presence of mind equal to any emergency, rising with the occasion, and an undaunted magnanimous bearing, and an energy and keenness which is but made intense by opposition. This is genius, this is heroism; it is the exhibition of a natural gift, which no culture can teach, at which no institution can aim: here, on the contrary, we are concerned, not with mere nature, but with training and teaching. That perfection of the intellect, which is the result of education, and its *beau ideal*, to be imparted to individuals in their respective measures, is the clear, calm, accurate vision and comprehension of all things, as far as the finite mind can embrace them, each in its place, and with its own characteristics upon it. It is almost prophetic from its knowledge of history; it is almost heart-searching from its knowledge of human nature; it has almost supernatural charity from its freedom from littleness and prejudice; it has almost the repose of faith, because nothing can startle it; it has almost the beauty and harmony of heavenly contemplation, so intimate is it with the eternal order of things and the music of the spheres.

And now, if I may take for granted that the true and adequate end of intellectual training and of a university is not learning or acquirement, but rather, is thought or reason exercised upon knowledge, or what may be called philosophy, I shall be in a position to explain the various mistakes which at the present day beset the subject of university education.

I say then, if we would improve the intellect, first of all, we must ascend; we cannot gain real knowledge on a level; we must generalise, we must reduce to method, we must have a grasp of principles, and group and shape our acquisitions by means of them. It matters not whether our field of operation be wide or limited; in every case, to command it, is to mount above it. Who has not felt the irritation of mind and impatience created by a deep, rich country, visited for the first time, with winding lanes, and high hedges, and green steeps, and tangled woods, and every thing smiling indeed, but in a maze? The same feeling comes upon us in a strange city, when we have no map of its streets. Hence you hear of practised travellers, when they first come into a place, mounting some high hill or church tower, by way of reconnoitering its neighbourhood. In like manner, you must be above your knowledge, not under it, or it will oppress you; and the more you have of it, the greater will be the load. The learning of a Salmasius or a

Burman, unless you are its master, will be your tyrant. *Imperat aut servit;* [16] if you can wield it with a strong arm, it is a great weapon; otherwise,

   Vis consili expers
Mole ruit suâ.[17]

You will be overwhelmed, like Tarpeia, by the heavy wealth which you have exacted from tributary generations.

Instances abound; there are authors who are as pointless as they are inexhaustible in their literary resources. They measure knowledge by bulk, as it lies in the rude block, without symmetry, without design. How many commentators are there on the classics, how many on Holy Scripture, from whom we rise up, wondering at the learning which has passed before us, and wondering why it passed! How many writers are there of Ecclesiastical history, such as Mosheim or Du Pin, who, breaking up their subject into details, destroy its life, and defraud us of the whole by their anxiety about the parts! The sermons, again, of the English divines in the seventeenth century, how often are they mere repertories of miscellaneous and officious learning! Of course Catholics also may read without thinking; and in their case, equally as with Protestants, it holds good, that such knowledge is unworthy of the name, knowledge which they have not thought through, and thought out. Such readers are only possessed by their knowledge, not possessed of it; nay, in matter of fact they are often even carried away by it, without any volition of their own. Recollect, the memory can tyrannise, as well as the imagination. Derangement, I believe, has been considered as a loss of control over the sequence of ideas. The mind, once set in motion, is henceforth deprived of the power of initiation, and becomes the victim of a train of associations, one thought suggesting another, in the way of cause and effect, as if by a mechanical process, or some physical necessity. No one, who has had experience of men of studious habits, but must recognise the existence of a parallel phenomenon in the case of those who have over-stimulated the memory. In such persons reason acts almost as feebly and as impotently as in the madman; once fairly started on any subject whatever, they have no power of self-control; they passively endure the succession of impulses which are evolved out of the original exciting cause; they are passed on from one idea to another and go steadily forward, plodding along one line of thought in spite of the amplest concessions of the hearer, or wandering from it in endless digression in spite of his remonstrances. Now, if, as is very certain, no one would envy the madman the glow and originality of his conceptions, why must we extol the cultivation of that intellect which is the prey, not indeed of barren fancies but of barren facts, of random intrusions from without, though not of morbid imaginations from within? And in thus speaking, I am not denying that a strong and ready memory is in itself a real treasure; I am not disparaging a well-stored mind, though it be nothing besides, provided it be sober, any more than I would despise a bookseller's shop:—it is of great value to others, even when not so to the owner. Nor am I banishing, far from it, the possessors of deep and multifarious learning from my ideal University; they adorn it in the eyes of men; I do but say that they constitute no type of the results at which it aims; that it is no great gain to the intellect to have enlarged the memory at the expense of faculties which are indisputably higher.

Nor indeed am I supposing that there is any great danger, at least in this day, of over-education; the danger is on the other side. I will tell you, gentlemen, what has been the practical error of the last twenty years,—not to load the memory of the student with a mass of undigested knowledge, but to force upon him so much that he has rejected all. It has been the error of distracting and enfeebling the mind by an unmeaning profusion of subjects; of implying that a smattering in a dozen branches of study is not shallowness, which it really is, but enlargement, which it is not; of considering an acquaintance with the learned names of things and persons and the possession of clever duodecimos, and attendance on eloquent lecturers, and membership with scientific institutions, and the sight of the experiments of a platform and the specimens of a museum, that all this was not dissipation of mind, but progress. All things now are to be learned at once, not first one thing, then another, not one well, but many badly. Learning is to be without exertion, without attention, without toil; without grounding, without advance, without finishing. There is to be nothing individual in it; and this, forsooth, is the wonder of the age. What the steam engine does with matter, the printing press is to do with the mind; it is to act mechanically, and the population is to be passively, almost unconsciously enlightened, by the mere multiplication and dissemination of volumes. Whether it be the school boy, or the school girl, or the youth at college, or the mechanic in the town, or the politician in the senate, all have been the victims in one way or other of this most preposterous and pernicious of delusions. Wise men have lifted up their voices in vain; and at length, lest their own institutions should be outshone and should disappear in the folly of the hour, they have been obliged, as far as they could with a good conscience, to humour a spirit which they could not withstand, and make temporising concessions at which they could not but inwardly smile.

It must not be supposed that, because I so speak, therefore I have some sort of fear of the education of the people: on the contrary, the more education they have, the better, so that it is really education. Nor am I an enemy to the cheap publication of scientific and literary works, which is now in vogue: on the contrary, I consider it a great advantage, convenience, and gain; that is, to those to whom education has given a capacity for using them. Further, I consider such innocent recreations as science and literature are able to furnish will be a very fit occupation of the thoughts and the leisure of young persons, and may be made the means of keeping them from bad employments and bad companions. Moreover, as to that superficial acquaintance with chemistry, and geology, and astronomy, and political economy, and modern history, and biography, and other branches of knowledge, which periodical literature and occasional lectures and scientific institutions diffuse through the community, I think it a graceful accomplishment, and a suitable, nay, in this day a necessary accomplishment, in the case of educated men. Nor, lastly, am I disparaging or discouraging the thorough acquisition of any one of these studies, or denying that, as far as it goes, such thorough acquisition is a real education of the mind. All I say is, call things by their right names, and do not confuse together ideas which are essentially different. A thorough knowledge of one science and a superficial acquaintance with many, are not the same thing; a smattering of a hundred things or a memory for detail, is not a philosophical or comprehensive view. Recreations are not education; accomplishments are not education. Do not say, the people must be educated, when, after all, you only mean amused, refreshed, soothed, put into good spirits and good humour, or kept from vicious excesses. I do not say that such amusements, such occupations of mind, are not a great gain; but they are not education. You may as well call drawing and fencing education as a general knowledge of botany or conchology. Stuffing birds or playing stringed instruments is an elegant pastime, and a resource to the idle, but it is not education; it does not form or cultivate the intellect. Education is a high word; it is the preparation for knowledge, and it is the imparting of knowledge in proportion to that preparation. We require intellectual eyes to know withal, as bodily eyes for sight. We need both objects and organs intellectual; we cannot gain them without setting about it; we cannot gain them in our sleep, or by haphazard. The best telescope does not dispense with eyes; the printing press or the lecture room will assist us greatly, but we must be true to ourselves, we must be parties in the work. A university is, according to the usual designation, an alma mater, knowing her children one by one, not a foundry, or a mint, or a treadmill.

I protest to you, gentlemen, that if I had to choose between a so-called university, which dispensed with residence and tutorial superintendence, and gave its degrees to any person who passed an examination in a wide range of subjects, and a university which had no professors or examinations at all, but merely brought a number of young men together for three or four years, and then sent them away as the University of Oxford is said to have done some sixty years since, if I were asked which of these two methods was the better discipline of the intellect,—mind, I do not say which is morally the better, for it is plain that compulsory study must be a good and idleness an intolerable mischief,—but if I must determine which of the two courses was the more successful in training, moulding, enlarging the mind, which sent out men the more fitted for their secular duties, which produced better public men, men of the world, men whose names would descend to posterity, I have no hesitation in giving the preference to that university which did nothing, over that which exacted of its members an acquaintance with every science under the sun. And, paradox as this may seem, still if results be the test of systems, the influence of the public schools and colleges of England, in the course of the last century, at least will bear out one side of the contrast as I have drawn it. What would come, on the other hand, of the ideal systems of education which have fascinated the imagination of this age, could they ever take effect, and whether they would not produce a generation frivolous, narrow-minded, and resourceless, intellectually considered, is a fair subject for debate; but so far is certain, that the universities and scholastic establishments, to which I refer, and which did little more than bring together first boys and then youths in large numbers, these institutions, with miserable deformities on the side of morals, with a hollow profession of Christianity, and a heathen code of ethics,—I say, at least they can boast of a succession of heroes and statesmen, of literary men and philosophers, of men conspicuous for great natural virtues, for habits of business, for knowledge of life, for practical judgment, for cultivated tastes, for accomplishments, who have made England what it is,—able to subdue the earth, able to domineer over Catholics.

How is this to be explained? I suppose as follows: When a multitude of young men, keen, open-hearted, sympathetic, and observant, as young men are, come together and freely mix with each other, they are sure to learn one from another, even if there be no one to teach them; the conversation of all is a series of lectures to each, and they gain for themselves new ideas and views, fresh matter of thought, and distinct principles for judging and acting, day by day. An infant has to learn the meaning of the information which its senses convey to it, and this seems to be its employment. It fancies all that the eye presents to it to be close to it, till it actually learns the contrary, and thus by practice does it ascertain the relations and uses of those first elements of knowledge which are necessary for its animal existence. A parallel teaching is necessary for our social being, and it is secured by a large school or a college; and this effect may be fairly called in its own department an enlargement of mind. It is seeing the world on a small field with little trouble; for the pupils or students come from very different places, and with widely different notions, and there is much to generalise, much to adjust, much to eliminate, there are inter-relations to be defined, and conventional rules to be established, in the process, by which the whole assemblage is moulded together, and gains one tone and one character.

Let it be clearly understood, I repeat it, that I am not taking into account moral or religious considerations; I am but saying that that youthful community will constitute a whole, it will embody a specific idea, it will represent a doctrine, it will administer a code of conduct, and it will furnish

Yet such is the better specimen of the fruit of that ambitious system which has of late years been making way among us: for its result on ordinary minds, and on the common run of students, is less satisfactory still; they leave their place of education simply dissipated and relaxed by the multiplicity of subjects, which they have never really mastered, and so shallow as not even to know their shallowness. How much better, I say, it is for the active and thoughtful intellect, where such is to be found, to eschew the college and the university altogether, than to submit to a drudgery so ignoble, a mockery so contumelious! How much more profitable for the independent mind, after the mere rudiments of education, to range through a library at random, taking down books as they meet him, and pursuing the trains of thought which his mother wit suggests! How much healthier to wander into the fields, and there with the exiled prince to find "tongues in the trees, books in the running brooks!" How much more genuine an education is that of the poor boy in the poem[19]—a poem, whether in conception or execution, one of the most touching in our language—who, not in the wide world, but ranging day by day around his widowed mother's home, "a dextrous gleaner" in a narrow field and with only such slender outfit

>   as the village school and books a few Supplied,

contrived from the beach, and the quay, and the fisher's boat, and the inn's fireside, and the tradesman's shop, and the shepherd's walk, and the smuggler's hut, and the mossy moor, and the screaming gulls, and the restless waves, to fashion for himself a philosophy and a poetry of his own!

But in a large subject, I am exceeding my necessary limits. Gentlemen, I must conclude abruptly; and postpone any summing up of my argument, should that be necessary, to another day.

FOOTNOTES:

[Footnote 11: Discourse VI in "The Idea of a University," 1852.]

[Footnote 12: Prima-facie: based on one's first impression.]

[Footnote 13: Four-square.]

[Footnote 14: To be moved by nothing.]

[Footnote 15: Happy is he who has come to know the sequences of things, and is thus above all fear and the dread march of fate and the roar of greedy Acheron.]

[Footnote 16: It rules or it serves.]

[Footnote 17: Brute force without intelligence falls by its own weight.]

[Footnote 18: Genius loci: spirit of the place.]

[Footnote 19: Crabbe's *Tales of the Hall.* This poem, let me say, I read on its first publication, above thirty years ago, with extreme delight, and have never lost my love of it; and on taking it up lately, found I was even more touched by it than heretofore. A work which can please in youth and age, seems to fulfil (in logical language) the *accidental definition* of a classic. (A further course of twenty years has passed, and I bear the same witness in favour of this poem.)]

LITERATURE AND SCIENCE[20]

MATTHEW ARNOLD

Practical people talk with a smile of Plato and of his absolute ideas; and it is impossible to deny that Plato's ideas do often seem unpractical and impracticable, and especially when one views them in connection with the life of a great workaday world like the United States. The necessary staple of the life of such a world Plato regards with disdain; handicraft and trade and the working professions he regards with disdain; but what becomes of the life of an industrial modern community if you take handicraft and trade and the working professions out of it? The base mechanic arts and handicrafts, says Plato, bring about a natural weakness in the principle of excellence in a man, so that he cannot govern the ignoble growths in him, but nurses them, and cannot understand fostering any other. Those who exercise such arts and trades, as they have their bodies, he says, marred by their vulgar businesses, so they have their souls, too, bowed and broken by them. And if one of these uncomely people has a mind to seek self-culture and philosophy, Plato compares him to a bald little tinker, who has scraped together money, and has got his release from service, and has had a bath, and bought a new coat, and is rigged out like a bridegroom about to marry the daughter of his master who has fallen into poor and helpless estate.

Nor do the working professions fare any better than trade at the hands of Plato. He draws for us an inimitable picture of the working lawyer, and of his life of bondage; he shows how this bondage from his youth up has stunted and warped him, and made him small and crooked of soul, encompassing him with difficulties which he is not man enough to rely on justice and truth as means to encounter, but has recourse, for help out of them, to falsehood and wrong. And so, says Plato, this poor creature is bent and broken, and grows up from boy to man without a particle of soundness in him, although exceedingly smart and clever in his own esteem.

One cannot refuse to admire the artist who draws these pictures. But we say to ourselves that his ideas show the influence of a primitive and obsolete order of things, when the warrior caste and the priestly caste were alone in honour, and the humble work of the world was done by slaves. We have now changed all that; the modern majority consists in work, as Emerson declares; and in work, we may add, principally of such plain and dusty kind as the work of cultivators of the ground, handicraftsmen, men of trade and business, men of the working professions. Above all is this true in a great industrious community such as that of the United States.

Now education, many people go on to say, is still mainly governed by the ideas of men like Plato, who lived when the warrior caste and the priestly or philosophical class were alone in honour, and the really useful part of the community were slaves. It is an education fitted for persons of leisure in such a community. This education passed from Greece and Rome to the feudal communities of Europe, where also the warrior caste and the priestly caste were alone held in honour, and where the really useful and working part of the community, though not nominally slaves as in the pagan world, were practically not much better off than slaves, and not more seriously regarded. And how absurd it is, people end by saying, to inflict this education upon an industrious modern community, where very few indeed are persons of leisure, and the mass to be considered has not leisure, but is bound, for its own great good, and for the great good of the world at large, to plain labour and to industrial pursuits, and the education in question tends necessarily to make men dissatisfied with these pursuits and unfitted for them!

That is what is said. So far I must defend Plato, as to plead that his view of education and studies is in the general, as it seems to me, sound enough, and fitted for all sorts and conditions of men, whatever their pursuits may be. "An intelligent man," says Plato, "will prize those studies which result in his soul getting soberness, righteousness, and wisdom, and will less value the others." I cannot consider *that* a bad description of the aim of education, and of the motives which should govern us in the choice of studies, whether we are preparing ourselves for a hereditary seat in the English House of Lords or for the pork trade in Chicago.

Still I admit that Plato's world was not ours, that his scorn of trade and handicraft is fantastic, that he had no conception of a great industrial community such as that of the United States, and that such a community must and will shape its education to suit its own needs. If the usual education handed down to it from the past does not suit it, it will certainly before long drop this and try another. The usual education in the past has been mainly literary. The question is whether the studies which were long supposed to be the best for all of us are practically the best now; whether others are not better. The tyranny of the past, many think, weighs on us injuriously in the predominance given to letters in education. The question is raised whether, to meet the needs of our modern life, the predominance ought not now to pass from letters to science; and naturally the question is nowhere raised with more energy than here in the United States. The design of abasing what is called "mere literary instruction and education," and of exalting what is called "sound, extensive, and practical scientific knowledge," is, in this intensely modern world of the United States, even more perhaps than in Europe, a very popular design, and makes great and rapid progress.

I am going to ask whether the present movement for ousting letters from their old predominance in education, and for transferring the predominance in education to the natural sciences; whether this brisk and flourishing movement ought to prevail, and whether it is likely that in the end it really will prevail. An objection may be raised which I will anticipate. My own studies have been almost wholly in letters, and my visits to the field of the natural sciences have been very slight and inadequate, although those sciences have always strongly moved my curiosity. A man of letters, it will perhaps be said, is not competent to discuss the comparative merits of letters and natural science as means of education. To this objection I reply, first of all, that his incompetence if he attempts the discussion but is really incompetent for it, will be abundantly visible; nobody will be taken in; he will have plenty of sharp observers and critics to save mankind from that danger. But the line I am going to follow is, as you will soon discover, so extremely simple, that perhaps it may be followed without failure even by one who for a more ambitious line of discussion would be quite incompetent.

Some of you may possibly remember a phrase of mine which has been the object of a good deal of comment; an observation to the effect that in our culture, the aim being *to know ourselves and the world*, we have, as the means to this end, *to know the best which has been thought and said in the world*. A man of science, who is also an excellent writer and the very prince of debaters, Professor Huxley, in a discourse at the opening of Sir Josiah Mason's College at Birmingham, laying hold of this phrase, expanded it by quoting some more words of mine, which are these: "The civilised world is to be regarded as now being, for intellectual and spiritual purposes, one great confederation, bound to a joint action and working to a common result; and whose members have for their proper outfit a knowledge of Greek, Roman, and Eastern antiquity, and of one another. Special local and temporary advantages being put out of account, that modern nation will in the intellectual and spiritual sphere make most progress, which most thoroughly carries out this programme."

Now on my phrase, thus enlarged, Professor Huxley remarks that when I speak of the above-mentioned knowledge as enabling us to know ourselves and the world, I assert *literature* to contain the materials which suffice for thus making us know ourselves and the world. But it is not by any means clear, says he, that after having learned all which ancient and modern literatures have to tell us, we have laid a sufficiently broad and deep foundation for that criticism of life, that knowledge of ourselves and the world, which constitutes culture. On the contrary, Professor Huxley declares that he finds himself "wholly unable to admit that either nations or individuals will really advance, if their outfit draws nothing from the stores of physical science. An army without weapons of precision, and with no particular base of operations, might more hopefully enter upon a campaign on the Rhine, than a man, devoid of a knowledge of what physical science has done in the last century, upon a criticism of life."

This shows how needful it is for those who are to discuss any matter together, to have a common understanding as to the sense of the terms they employ,—how needful, and how difficult. What Professor Huxley says, implies just the reproach which is so often brought against the study of *belles lettres*, as they are called: that the study is an elegant one, but slight and ineffectual; a smattering of Greek and Latin and other ornamental things, of little use for any one whose object is to get at truth, and to be a practical man. So, too, M. Renan talks of the "superficial humanism" of a school course which treats us as if we were all going to be poets, writers, preachers, orators, and he opposes this humanism to positive science, or the critical search after truth. And there is always a tendency in those who are remonstrating against the predominance of letters in education, to understand by letters *belles lettres*, and by *belles lettres* a superficial humanism, the opposite of science or true knowledge.

But when we talk of knowing Greek and Roman antiquity, for instance, which is the knowledge people have called the humanities, I for my part mean a knowledge which is something more than a superficial humanism, mainly decorative. "I call all teaching *scientific*," says Wolf, the critic of Homer, "which is systematically laid out and followed up to its original sources. For example: a knowledge of classical antiquity is scientific when the remains of classical antiquity are correctly studied in the original languages." There can be no doubt that Wolf is perfectly right; that all learning is scientific which is systematically laid out and followed up to its original sources, and that a genuine humanism is scientific.

When I speak of knowing Greek and Roman antiquity, therefore, as a help to knowing ourselves and the world, I mean more than a knowledge of so much vocabulary, so much grammar, so many portions of authors in the Greek and Latin languages; I mean knowing the Greeks and Romans, and their life and genius, and what they were and did in the world; what we get from them, and what is its value: That, at least, is the ideal; and when we talk of endeavouring to know Greek and Roman antiquity, as a help to knowing ourselves and the world, we mean endeavouring so to know them as to satisfy this ideal, however much we may still fall short of it.

The same also as to knowing our own and other modern nations, with the like aim of getting to understand ourselves and the world. To know the best that has been thought and said by the modern nations, is to know, says Professor Huxley, "only what modern *literatures* have to tell us; it is the criticism of life contained in modern literature." And yet "the distinctive character of our times," he urges, "lies in the vast and constantly increasing part which is played by natural knowledge." And how, therefore, can a man, devoid of knowledge of what physical science has done in the last century, enter hopefully upon a criticism of modern life?

Let us, I say, be agreed about the meaning of the terms we are using. I talk of knowing the best which has been thought and uttered in the world; Professor Huxley says this means knowing *literature.* Literature is a large word; it may mean everything written with letters or printed in a book. Euclid's *Elements* and Newton's *Principia* are thus literature. All knowledge that reaches us through books is literature. But by literature Professor Huxley means *belles lettres.* He means to make me say, that knowing the best which has been thought and said by the modern nations is knowing their *belles lettres* and no more. And this is no sufficient equipment, he argues, for a criticism of modern life. But as I do not mean, by knowing ancient Rome, knowing merely more or less of Latin *belles lettres*, and taking no account of Rome's military, and political, and legal, and administrative work in the world; and as, by knowing ancient Greece, I understand knowing her as the giver of Greek art, and the guide to a free and right use of reason and to scientific method, and the founder of our mathematics and physics and astronomy and biology,—I understand knowing her as all this, and not merely knowing certain Greek poems, and histories, and treatises, and speeches,—so as to the knowledge of modern nations also. By knowing modern nations, I mean not merely knowing their *belles lettres*, but knowing also what has been done by such men as Copernicus, Galileo, Newton, Darwin. "Our ancestors learned," says Professor Huxley, "that the earth is the centre of the visible universe, and that man is the cynosure of things terrestrial; and more especially was it inculcated that the course of nature has no fixed order, but that it could be, and constantly was, altered." But for us now, continues Professor Huxley, "the notions of the beginning and the end of the world entertained by our forefathers are no longer credible. It is very certain that the earth is not the chief body in the material universe, and that the world is not subordinated to man's use. It is even more certain that nature is the expression of a definite order, with which nothing interferes." "And yet," he cries, "the purely classical education advocated by the representatives of the humanists in our day gives no inkling of all this!"

In due place and time I will just touch upon that vexed question of classical education; but at present the question is as to what is meant by knowing the best which modern nations have thought and said. It is not knowing their *belles lettres* merely which is meant. To know Italian *belles lettres* is not to know Italy, and to know English *belles lettres* is not to know England. Into knowing Italy and England there comes a great deal more, Galileo and Newton amongst it. The reproach of being a superficial humanism, a tincture of *belles lettres*, may attach rightly enough to some other disciplines; but to the particular discipline recommended when I proposed knowing the best that has been thought and said in the world, it does not apply. In that best I certainly include what in modern times has been thought and said by the great observers and knowers of nature.

There is, therefore, really no question between Professor Huxley and me as to whether knowing the great results of the modern scientific study of nature is not required as a part of our culture, as well as knowing the products of literature and art. But to follow the processes by which those results are reached, ought, say the friends of physical science, to be made the staple of education for the bulk of mankind. And here there does arise a question between those whom Professor Huxley calls with playful sarcasm "the Levites of culture," and those whom the poor humanist is sometimes apt to regard as its Nebuchadnezzars.

The great results of the scientific investigation of nature we are agreed upon knowing, but how much of our study are we bound to give to the processes by which those results are reached? The results have their visible bearing on human life. But all the processes, too, all the items of fact by which those results are reached and established, are interesting. All knowledge is interesting to a wise man, and the knowledge of nature is interesting to all men. It is very interesting to know, that, from the albuminous white of the egg, the chick in the egg gets the materials for its flesh, bones, blood, and feathers; while, from the fatty yolk of the egg, it gets the heat and energy which enable it at length to break its shell and begin the world. It is less interesting, perhaps, but still it is interesting, to know that when a taper burns, the wax is converted into carbonic acid and water. Moreover, it is quite true that the habit of dealing with facts, which is given by the study of nature, is, as the friends of physical science praise it for being, an excellent discipline. The appeal, in the study of nature, is constantly to observation and experiment; not only is it said that the thing is so, but we can be made to see that it is so. Not only does a man tell us that when a taper burns the wax is converted into carbonic acid and water, as a man may tell us, if he likes, that Charon is punting his ferry boat on the river Styx, or that Victor Hugo is a sublime poet, or Mr. Gladstone the most admirable of statesmen; but we are made to see that the conversion into carbonic acid and water does actually happen. This reality of natural knowledge it is, which makes the friends of physical science contrast it, as a knowledge of things, with the humanist's knowledge, which is, they say, a knowledge of words. And hence Professor Huxley is moved to lay it down that, "for the purpose of attaining real culture, an exclusively scientific education is at least as effectual as an exclusively literary education." And a certain President of the Section for Mechanical Science in the British Association is, in Scripture phrase, "very bold," and declares that if a man, in his mental training, "has substituted literature and history for natural science, he has chosen the less useful alternative." But whether we go these lengths or not, we must all admit that in natural science the habit gained of dealing with facts is a most valuable discipline, and that every one should have some experience of it.

More than this, however, is demanded by the reformers. It is proposed to make the training in natural science the main part of education, for the great majority of mankind at any rate. And here, I confess, I part company with the friends of physical science, with whom up to this point I have been agreeing. In differing from them, however, I wish to proceed with the utmost caution and diffidence. The smallness of my own acquaintance with the disciplines of natural science is ever before my mind, and I am fearful of doing these disciplines an injustice. The ability and pugnacity of the partisans of natural science make them formidable persons to contradict. The tone of tentative inquiry, which befits a being of dim faculties and bounded knowledge, is the tone I would wish to take and not to depart from. At present it seems to me, that those who are for giving to natural knowledge, as they call it, the chief place in the education of the majority of mankind, leave one important thing out of their account: the constitution of human nature. But I put this forward on the strength of some facts not at all recondite, very far from it; facts capable of being stated in the simplest possible fashion, and to which, if I so state them, the man of science will, I am sure, be willing to allow their due weight.

Deny the facts altogether, I think, he hardly can. He can hardly deny, that when we set ourselves to enumerate the powers which go to the building up of human life, and say that they are the power of conduct, the power of intellect and knowledge, the power of beauty, and the power of social life and manners—he can hardly deny that this scheme, though drawn in rough and plain lines enough, and not pretending to scientific exactness, does yet give a fairly true representation of the matter. Human nature is built up by these powers; we have the need for them all. When we have rightly met and adjusted the claims of them all, we shall then be in a fair way for getting soberness and righteousness, with wisdom. This is evident enough, and the friends of physical science would admit it.

But perhaps they may not have sufficiently observed another thing: namely, that the several powers just mentioned are not isolated, but there is, in the generality of mankind, a perpetual tendency to relate them one to another in divers ways. With one such way of relating them I am particularly concerned now. Following our instinct for intellect and knowledge, we acquire pieces of knowledge; and presently, in the generality of men, there arises the desire to relate these pieces of knowledge to our sense for conduct, to our sense for beauty,—and there is weariness and dissatisfaction if the desire is balked. Now in this desire lies, I think, the strength of that hold which letters have upon us.

All knowledge is, as I said just now, interesting; and even items of knowledge which from the nature of the case cannot well be related, but must stand isolated in our thoughts, have their interest. Even lists of exceptions have their interest. If we are studying Greek accents, it is interesting to know that *pais* and *pas*, and some other monosyllables of the same form of declension, do not take the circumflex upon the last syllable of the genitive plural, but vary, in this respect, from the common rule. If we are studying physiology, it is interesting to know that the pulmonary artery carries dark blood and the pulmonary vein carries bright blood, departing in this respect from the common rule, for the division of labour between the veins and the arteries. But every one knows how we seek naturally to combine the pieces of our knowledge together, to bring them under general rules, to relate them to principles; and how unsatisfactory and tiresome it would be to go on forever learning lists of exceptions, or accumulating items of fact which must stand isolated.

Well, that same need of relating our knowledge, which operates here within the sphere of our knowledge itself, we shall find operating, also, outside that sphere. We experience, as we go on learning and knowing,—the vast majority of us experience,—the need of relating what we have learned and known to the sense which we have in us for conduct, to the sense which we have in us for beauty.

A certain Greek prophetess of Mantineia in Arcadia, Diotima by name, once explained to the philosopher Socrates that love, and impulse, and bent of all kinds, is, in fact, nothing else but the desire in men that good should forever be present to them. This desire for good, Diotima assured Socrates, is our fundamental desire, of which fundamental desire every impulse in us is only some one particular form. And therefore this fundamental desire it is, I suppose,—this desire in men that good should be forever present to them,—which acts in us when we feel the impulse for relating our knowledge to our sense for conduct and to our sense for beauty. At any rate, with men in general the instinct exists. Such is human nature. And the instinct, it will be admitted, is innocent, and human nature is preserved by our following the lead of its innocent instincts. Therefore, in seeking to gratify this instinct in question, we are following the instinct of self-preservation in humanity.

But, no doubt, some kinds of knowledge cannot be made to directly serve the instinct in question, cannot be directly related to the sense for beauty, to the sense for conduct. These are instrument-knowledges; they lead on to other knowledges, which can. A man who passes his life in instrument-knowledges is a specialist. They may be invaluable as instruments to something beyond, for those who have the gift thus to employ them; and they may be disciplines in themselves wherein it is useful for every one to have some schooling. But it is inconceivable that the generality of men should pass all their mental life with Greek accents or with formal logic.

My friend Professor Sylvester, who is one of the first mathematicians in the world, holds transcendental doctrines as to the virtue of mathematics, but those doctrines are not for common men. In the very Senate House and heart of our English Cambridge I once ventured, though not without an apology for my profaneness, to hazard the opinion that for the majority of mankind a little of mathematics, even, goes a long way. Of course this is quite consistent with their being of immense importance as an instrument to something else; but it is the few who have the aptitude for thus using them, not the bulk of mankind.

The natural sciences do not, however, stand on the same footing with these instrument-knowledges. Experience shows us that the generality of men will find more interest in learning that, when a taper burns, the wax is converted into carbonic acid and water, or in learning the explanation of the phenomenon of dew, or in learning how the circulation of the blood is carried on, than they find in learning that the genitive plural of *pais* and *pas* does not take the circumflex on the termination. And one piece of natural knowledge is added to another, and others are added to that, and at last we come to propositions so interesting as Mr. Darwin's famous proposition that "our ancestor was a hairy quadruped furnished with a tail and pointed ears, probably arboreal in his habits." Or we come to propositions of such reach and magnitude as those which Professor Huxley delivers, when he says that the notions of our forefathers about the beginning and the end of the world were all wrong and that nature is the expression of a definite order with which nothing interferes.

Interesting, indeed, these results of science are, important they are, and we should all of us be acquainted with them. But what I now wish you to mark is, that we are still, when they are propounded to us and we receive them, we are still in the sphere of intellect and knowledge. And for the generality of men there will be found, I say, to arise, when they have duly taken in the proposition that their ancestor was "a hairy quadruped furnished with a tail and pointed ears, probably arboreal in his habits," there will be found to arise an invincible desire to relate this proposition to the sense in us for conduct, and to the sense in us for beauty. But this the men of science will not do for us, and will hardly even profess to do. They will give us other pieces of knowledge, other facts, about other animals and their ancestors, or about plants, or about stones, or about stars; and they may finally bring us to those great "general conceptions of the universe, which are forced upon us all," says Professor Huxley, "by the progress of physical science." But still it will be *knowledge* only which they give us; knowledge not put for us into relation with our sense for conduct, our sense for beauty, and touched with emotion by being so put; not thus put for us, and therefore, to the majority of mankind, after a certain while, unsatisfying, wearying.

Not to the born naturalist, I admit. But what do we mean by a born naturalist? We mean a man in whom the zeal for observing nature is so uncommonly strong and eminent, that it marks him off from the bulk of mankind. Such a man will pass his life happily in collecting natural knowledge and reasoning upon it, and will ask for nothing, or hardly anything, more. I have heard it said that the sagacious and admirable naturalist whom we lost not very long ago, Mr. Darwin, once owned to a friend that for his part he did not experience the necessity for two things which most men find so necessary to them,—religion and poetry; science and the domestic affections, he thought, were enough. To a born naturalist, I can well understand that this should seem so. So absorbing is his occupation with nature, so strong his love for his occupation, that he goes on acquiring natural knowledge and reasoning upon it, and has little time or inclination for thinking about getting it related to the desire in man for conduct, the desire in man for beauty. He relates it to them for himself as he goes along, so far as he feels the need; and he draws from the domestic affections all the additional solace necessary. But then Darwins are extremely rare. Another great and admirable master of natural knowledge, Faraday, was a Sandemanian. That is to say, he related his knowledge to his instinct for conduct and to his instinct for beauty, by the aid of that respectable Scottish sectary, Robert Sandeman. And so strong, in general, is the demand of religion and poetry to have their share in a man, to associate themselves with his knowing, and to relieve and rejoice it, that probably, for one man amongst us with the disposition to do as Darwin did in this respect, there are at least fifty with the disposition to do as Faraday.

Education lays hold upon us, in fact, by satisfying this demand. Professor Huxley holds up to scorn mediaeval education, with its neglect of the knowledge of nature, its poverty even of literary studies, its formal logic devoted to "showing how and why that which the Church said was true must be true." But the great mediaeval universities were not brought into being, we may be sure, by the zeal for giving a jejune and contemptible education. Kings have been their nursing fathers, and queens have been their nursing mothers, but not for this. The mediaeval universities came into being, because the supposed knowledge, delivered by Scripture and the Church, so deeply engaged men's hearts, by so simply, easily, and powerfully relating itself to their desire for conduct, their desire for beauty. All other knowledge was dominated by this supposed knowledge and was subordinated to it, because of the surpassing strength of the hold which it gained upon the affections of men, by allying itself profoundly with their sense for conduct, their sense for beauty.

But now, says Professor Huxley, conceptions of the universe fatal to the notions held by our forefathers have been forced upon us by physical science. Grant to him that they are thus fatal, that the new conceptions must and will soon become current everywhere, and that every one will finally perceive them to be fatal to the beliefs of our forefathers. The need of humane letters, as they are truly called, because they serve the paramount desire in men that good should be forever present to them,—the need of humane letters to establish a relation between the new conceptions, and our instinct for beauty, our instinct for conduct, is only the more visible. The middle age could do without humane letters, as it could do without the study of nature, because its supposed knowledge was made to engage its emotions so powerfully. Grant that the supposed knowledge disappears, its power of being made to engage the emotions will of course disappear along with it,—but the emotions themselves, and their claim to be engaged and satisfied, will remain. Now if we find by experience that humane letters have an undeniable power of engaging the emotions, the importance of humane letters in a man's training becomes not less, but greater, in proportion to the success of modern science in extirpating what it calls "mediaeval thinking."

Have humane letters, then, have poetry and eloquence, the power here attributed to them of engaging the emotions, and do they exercise it? And if they have it and exercise it, *how* do they exercise it, so as to exert an influence upon man's sense for conduct, his sense for beauty? Finally, even if they both can and do exert an influence upon the senses in question, how are they to relate to them the results,—the modern results,—of natural science? All these questions may be asked. First, have poetry and eloquence the power of calling out the emotions? The appeal is to experience. Experience shows that for the vast majority of men, for mankind in general, they have the power. Next, do they exercise it? They do. But then, *how* do they exercise it so as to affect man's sense for conduct, his sense for beauty? And this is perhaps a case for applying the Preacher's words: "Though a man labor to seek it out, yet he shall not find it; yea, further, though a wise man think to know it, yet shall he not be able to find it."[21] Why should it be one thing, in its effect upon the emotions, to say, "Patience is a virtue," and quite another thing, in its effect upon the emotions, to say with Homer,

[Greek: tlaeton gar Moirai thumon thesan anthropoisin—[22]]

"for an enduring heart have the destinies appointed to the children of men"? Why should it be one thing, in its effect upon the emotions, to say with philosopher Spinoza, *Felicitas in eo consistit quod homo suum esse conservare potest*—"Man's happiness consists in his being able to preserve his own essence," and quite another thing, in its effect upon the emotions, to say with the Gospel, "What is a man advantaged, if he gain the whole world, and lose himself, forfeit himself?" How does this difference of effect arise? I cannot tell, and I am not much concerned to know; the important thing is that it does arise, and that we can profit by it. But how, finally, are poetry and eloquence to exercise the power of relating the modern results of natural science to man's instinct for conduct, his instinct for beauty? And here again I answer that I do not know *how* they will exercise it, but that they can and will exercise it I am sure. I do not mean that modern philosophical poets and modern philosophical moralists are to come and relate for us, in express terms, the results of modern scientific research to our instinct for conduct, our instinct for beauty. But I mean that we shall find, as a matter of experience, if we know the best that has been thought and uttered in the world, we shall find that the art and poetry and eloquence of men who lived, perhaps, long ago, who had the most limited natural knowledge, who had the most erroneous conceptions about many important matters, we shall find that this art, and poetry, and eloquence, have in fact not only the power of refreshing and delighting us, they have also the power,—such is the strength and worth, in essentials, of their authors' criticism of life,—they have a fortifying, and elevating, and quickening, and suggestive power, capable of wonderfully helping us to relate the results of modern science to our need for conduct, our need for beauty. Homer's conceptions of the physical universe were, I imagine, grotesque; but really, under the shock of hearing from modern science that "the world is not subordinated to man's use, and that man is not the cynosure of things terrestrial," I could, for my own part, desire no better comfort than Homer's line which I quoted just now,

[Greek: tlaeton gar Moirai thumon thesan anthropoisin—]

"for an enduring heart have the destinies appointed to the children of men!"

And the more that men's minds are cleared, the more that the results of science are frankly accepted, the more that poetry and eloquence come to be received and studied as what in truth they really are,—the criticism of life by gifted men, alive and active with extraordinary power at an unusual number of points;—so much the more will the value of humane letters, and of art also, which is an utterance having a like kind of power with theirs, be felt and acknowledged, and their place in education be secured.

Let us therefore, all of us, avoid indeed as much as possible any invidious comparison between the merits of humane letters, as means of education, and the merits of the natural sciences. But when some President of a Section for Mechanical Science insists on making the comparison, and tells us that "he who in his training has substituted literature and history for natural science has chosen the less useful alternative," let us make answer to him that the student of humane letters only, will, at least, know also the great general conceptions brought in by modern physical science; for science, as Professor Huxley says, forces them upon us all. But the student of the natural sciences only, will, by our very hypothesis, know nothing of humane letters; not to mention that in setting himself to be perpetually accumulating natural knowledge, he sets himself to do what only specialists have in general the gift for doing genially. And so he will probably be unsatisfied, or at any rate incomplete, and even more incomplete than the student of humane letters only.

I once mentioned in a school report, how a young man in one of our English training colleges having to paraphrase the passage in *Macbeth* beginning,

Canst thou not minister to a mind diseased?

turned this line into, "Can you not wait upon the lunatic?" And I remarked what a curious state of things it would be, if every pupil of our national schools knew, let us say, that the moon is two thousand one hundred and sixty miles in diameter, and thought at the same time that a good paraphrase for

Canst thou not minister to a mind diseased?

was, "Can you not wait upon the lunatic?" If one is driven to choose, I think I would rather have a young person ignorant about the moon's diameter, but aware that "Can you not wait upon the lunatic?" is bad, than a young person whose education had been such as to manage things the other way.

Or to go higher than the pupils of our national schools. I have in my mind's eye a member of our British Parliament who comes to travel here in America, who afterwards relates his travels, and who shows a really masterly knowledge of the geology of this great country and of its mining capabilities, but who ends by gravely suggesting that the United States should borrow a prince from our Royal Family, and should make him their king, and should create a House of Lords of great landed proprietors after the pattern of ours; and then America, he thinks, would have her future happily and perfectly secured. Surely, in this case, the President of the Section for Mechanical Science would himself hardly say that our member of Parliament, by concentrating himself upon geology and mineralogy, and so on, and not attending to literature and history, had "chosen the more useful alternative."

If then there is to be separation and option between humane letters on the one hand, and the natural sciences on the other, the great majority of mankind, all who have not exceptional and overpowering aptitudes for the study of nature, would do well, I cannot but think, to choose to be educated in humane letters rather than in the natural sciences. Letters will call out their being at more points, will make them live more.

I said that before I ended I would just touch on the question of classical education, and I will keep my word. Even if literature is to retain a large place in our education, yet Latin and Greek, say the friends of progress, will certainly have to go. Greek is the grand offender in the eyes of these gentlemen. The attackers of the established course of study think that against Greek, at any rate, they have irresistible arguments. Literature may perhaps be needed in education, they say; but why on earth should it be Greek literature? Why not French or German? Nay, "has not an Englishman models in his own literature of every kind of excellence?" As before, it is not on any weak pleadings of my own that I rely for convincing the gainsayers; it is on the constitution of human nature itself, and on the instinct of self-preservation in humanity. The instinct for beauty is set in human nature, as surely as the instinct for knowledge is set there, or the instinct for conduct. If the instinct for beauty is served by Greek literature and art as it is served by no other literature and art, we may trust to the instinct of self-preservation in humanity for keeping Greek as part of our culture. We may trust to it for even making the study of Greek more prevalent than it is now. Greek will come, I hope, some day to be studied more rationally than at present; but it will be increasingly studied as men increasingly feel the need in them for beauty, and how powerfully Greek art and Greek literature can serve this need. Women will again study Greek, as

Lady Jane Grey did; I believe that in that chain of forts, with which the fair host of the Amazons are now engirdling our English universities,—I find that here in America, in colleges like Smith College in Massachusetts, and Vassar College in the State of New York, and in the happy families of the mixed universities out West,—they are studying it already.

Defuit una mihi symmetria prisca,—"The antique symmetry was the one thing wanting to me," said Leonardo da Vinci; and he was an Italian. I will not presume to speak for the Americans, but I am sure that, in the Englishman, the want of this admirable symmetry of the Greeks is a thousand times more great and crying than in any Italian. The results of the want show themselves most glaringly, perhaps, in our architecture, but they show themselves, also, in all our art. *Fit details strictly combined, in view of a large general result nobly conceived*; that is just the beautiful *symmetria prisca* of the Greeks, and it is just where we English fail, where all our art fails. Striking ideas we have, and well-executed details we have; but that high symmetry which, with satisfying and delightful effect, combines them, we seldom or never have. The glorious beauty of the Acropolis at Athens did not come from single fine things stuck about on that hill, a statue here, a gateway there;—no, it arose from all things being perfectly combined for a supreme total effect. What must not an Englishman feel about our deficiencies in this respect, as the sense for beauty, whereof this symmetry is an essential element, awakens and strengthens within him! what will not one day be his respect and desire for Greece and its *symmetria prisca,* when the scales drop from his eyes as he walks the London streets, and he sees such a lesson in meanness as the Strand, for instance, in its true deformity! But here we are coming to our friend Mr. Ruskin's province, and I will not intrude upon it, for he is its very sufficient guardian.

And so we at last find, it seems, we find flowing in favor of the humanities the natural and necessary stream of things, which seemed against them when we started. The "hairy quadruped furnished with a tail and pointed ears, probably arboreal in his habits," this good fellow carried hidden in his nature, apparently, something destined to develop into a necessity for humane letters. Nay, more: we seem finally to be even led to the further conclusion that our hairy ancestor carried in his nature, also, a necessity for Greek.

And therefore, to say the truth, I cannot really think that humane letters are in much actual danger of being thrust out from their leading place in education, in spite of the array of authorities against them at this moment. So long as human nature is what it is, their attractions will remain irresistible. As with Greek, so with letters generally: they will some day come, we may hope, to be studied more rationally, but they will not lose their place. What will happen will rather be that there will be crowded into education other matters besides, far too many; there will be, perhaps, a period of unsettlement and confusion and false tendency; but letters will not in the end lose their leading place. If they lose it for a time, they will get it back again. We shall be brought back to them by our wants and aspirations. And a poor humanist may possess his soul in patience, neither strive nor cry, admit the energy and brilliancy of the partisans of physical science, and their present favor with the public, to be far greater than his own, and still have a happy faith that the nature of things works silently on behalf of the studies which he loves, and that, while we shall all have to acquaint ourselves with the great results reached by modern science, and to give ourselves as much training in its disciplines as we can conveniently carry, yet the majority of men will always require humane letters; and so much the more, as they have the more and the greater results of science to relate to the need in man for conduct, and to the need in him for beauty.

FOOTNOTES:

[Footnote 20: From "Discourses in America," 1885.]

[Footnote 21: From Ecclesiastes, viii. 17.]

[Footnote 22: From the "Iliad," xxiv. 49.]

HOW TO READ[23]

FREDERIC HARRISON

It is the fashion for those who have any connection with letters to expatiate on the infinite blessings of literature, and the miraculous achievements of the press: to extol, as a gift above price, the taste for study and the love of reading. Far be it from me to gainsay the inestimable value of good books, or to discourage any man from reading the best; but I often think that we forget that other side to this glorious view of literature—the misuse of books, the debilitating waste of brain in aimless, promiscuous, vapid reading, or even, it may be, in the poisonous inhalation of mere literary garbage and bad men's worst thoughts.

For what can a book be more than the man who wrote it? The brightest genius seldom puts the best of his own soul into his printed page; and some famous men have certainly put the worst of theirs. Yet are all men desirable companions, much less teachers, able to give us advice, even of those who get reputation and command a hearing? To put out of the question that writing which is positively bad, are we not, amidst the multiplicity of books and of writers, in continual danger of being drawn off by what is stimulating rather than solid, by curiosity after something accidentally notorious, by what has no intelligible thing to recommend it, except that it is new? Now, to stuff our minds with what is simply trivial, simply curious, or that which at best has but a low nutritive power, this is to close our minds to what is solid and enlarging, and spiritually sustaining. Whether our neglect of the great books comes from our not reading at all, or from an incorrigible habit of reading the little books, it ends in just the same thing. And that thing is ignorance of all the greater literature of the world. To neglect all the abiding parts of knowledge for the sake of the evanescent parts is really to know nothing worth knowing. It is in the end the same, whether we do not use our minds for serious study at all, or whether we exhaust them by an impotent voracity for desultory "information"—a thing as fruitful as whistling. Of the two evils I prefer the former. At least, in that case, the mind is healthy and open. It is not gorged and enfeebled by excess in that which cannot nourish, much less enlarge and beautify our nature.

But there is much more than this. Even to those who resolutely avoid the idleness of reading what is trivial, a difficulty is presented—a difficulty every day increasing by virtue even of our abundance of books. What are the subjects, what are the class of books we are to read, in what order, with what connection, to what ultimate use or object? Even those who are resolved to read the better books are embarrassed by a field of choice practically boundless. The longest life, the greatest industry, joined to the most powerful memory, would not suffice to make us profit from a hundredth part of the world of books before us. If the great Newton said that he seemed to have been all his life gathering a few shells on the shore, whilst a boundless ocean of truth still lay beyond and unknown to him, how much more to each of us must the sea of literature be a pathless immensity beyond our powers of vision or of reach—an immensity in which industry itself is useless without judgment, method, discipline; where it is of infinite importance what we can learn and remember, and of utterly no importance what we may have once looked at or heard of. Alas! the most of our reading leaves as little mark even in our own education as the foam that gathers round the keel of a passing boat! For myself, I am inclined to think the most useful help to reading is to know what we should not read, what we can keep out from that small cleared spot in the overgrown jungle of "information," the corner which we can call our ordered patch of fruit-bearing knowledge. The incessant accumulation of fresh books must hinder any real knowledge of the old; for the multiplicity of volumes becomes a bar upon our use of any. In literature especially does it hold—that we cannot see the wood for the trees.

How shall we choose our books? Which are the best, the eternal, indispensable books? To all to whom reading is something more than a refined idleness these questions recur, bringing with them the sense of bewilderment; and a still, small voice within us is for ever crying out for some guide across the Slough of Despond of an illimitable and ever-swelling literature. How many a man stands beside it, as uncertain of his pathway as the Pilgrim, when he who dreamed the immortal dream heard him "break out with a lamentable cry; saying, what shall I do?"

And this, which comes home to all of us at times, presses hardest upon those who have lost the opportunity of systematic education, who have to educate themselves, or who seek to guide the education of their young people. Systematic reading is but little in favour even amongst studious men; in a true sense it is hardly possible for women. A comprehensive course of home study, and a guide to books, fit for the highest education of women, is yet a blank page remaining to be filled. Generations of men of culture have laboured to organise a system of reading and materials appropriate for the methodical education of men in academic lines. Teaching equal in mental calibre to any that is open to men in universities, yet modified for the needs of those who must study at home, remains in the dim pages of that melancholy volume entitled *Libri valde desiderati*.[24]

I do not aspire to fill one of those blank pages; but I long to speak a word or two, as the Pilgrim did to Neighbour Pliable, upon the glories that await those who will pass through the narrow wicket-gate. On this, if one can find anything useful to say, it may be chiefly from the memory of the waste labour and pitiful stumbling in the dark which fill up so much of the travail that one is fain to call one's own education. We who have wandered in the wastes so long, and lost so much of our lives in our wandering, may at least offer warnings to younger wayfarers, as men who in thorny paths have borne the heat and burden of the day might give a clue to their journey to those who have yet a morning and a noon. As I look back and think of those cataracts of printed stuff which honest compositors set up, meaning, let us trust, no harm, and which at least found them in daily bread,—printed stuff which I and the rest of us, to our infinitely small profit, have consumed with our eyes, not even making an honest living of it, but much impairing our substance,—I could almost reckon the printing press as amongst the scourges of mankind. I am grown a wiser and a sadder man, importunate, like that Ancient Mariner, to tell each blithe wedding guest the tale of his shipwreck on the infinite sea of printers' ink, as one escaped by mercy and grace from the region where there is water, water, everywhere, and not a drop to drink.

A man of power, who has got more from books than most of his contemporaries, once said: "Form a habit of reading, do not mind what you read; the reading of better books will come when you have a habit of reading the inferior." We need not accept this *obiter dictum*[25] of Lord Sherbrooke. A habit of reading idly debilitates and corrupts the mind for all wholesome reading; the habit of reading wisely is one of the most difficult habits to acquire, needing strong resolution and infinite pains; and reading for mere reading's sake, instead of for the sake of the good we gain from reading, is one of the worst and commonest and most unwholesome habits we have. And so our inimitable humorist has made delightful fun of the solid books,—which no gentleman's library should be without,—the Humes, Gibbons, Adam Smiths, which, he says, are not books at all, and prefers some "kindhearted play-book," or at times the *Town and County Magazine*. Poor Lamb has not a little to answer for, in the revived relish for garbage unearthed from old theatrical dungheaps. Be it jest or earnest, I have little patience with the Elia-tic philosophy of the frivolous. Why do we still suffer the traditional hypocrisy about the dignity of literature—literature, I mean, in the gross, which includes about equal parts of what is useful and what is useless? Why are books as books, writers as writers, readers as readers, meritorious, apart from any good in them, or anything that we can get from them? Why do we pride ourselves on our powers of absorbing print, as our grandfathers did on their gifts in imbibing port, when we know that there is a mode of absorbing print which makes it impossible that we can ever learn anything good out of books?

Our stately Milton said in a passage which is one of the watchwords of the English race, "as good almost kill a Man as kill a good Book." But has he not also said that he would "have a vigilant eye how Bookes demeane themselves, as well as men; and do sharpest justice on them as malefactors"?... Yes! they do kill the good book who deliver up their few and precious hours of reading to the trivial book; they make it dead for them; they do what lies in them to destroy "the precious life-blood of a master-spirit, imbalm'd and treasured up on purpose to a life beyond life;" they "spill that season'd life of man preserv'd and stor'd up in Bookes." For in the wilderness of books most men, certainly all busy men, *must* strictly choose. If they saturate their minds with the idler books, the "good book," which Milton calls "an immortality rather than a life," is dead to them: it is a book sealed up and buried.

It is most right that in the great republic of letters there should be freedom of intercourse and a spirit of equality. Every reader who holds a book in his hand is free of the inmost minds of men past and present; their lives both within and without the pale of their uttered thoughts are unveiled to him; he needs no introduction to the greatest; he stands on no ceremony with them; he may, if he be so minded, scribble "doggrel" on his Shelley, or he may kick Lord Byron, if he please, into a corner. He hears Burke perorate, and Johnson dogmatise, and Scott tell his border tales, and Wordsworth muse on the hillside, without the leave of any man, or the payment of any toll. In the republic of letters there are no privileged orders or places reserved. Every man who has written a book, even the diligent Mr. Whitaker, is in one sense an author; "a book's a book although there's nothing in't;" and every man who can decipher a penny journal is in one sense a reader. And your "general reader," like the grave-digger in Hamlet, is hail-fellow with all the mighty dead; he pats the skull of the jester; batters the cheek of lord, lady, or courtier; and uses "imperious Caesar" to teach boys the Latin declensions.

But this noble equality of all writers—of all writers and of all readers—has a perilous side to it. It is apt to make us indiscriminate in the books we read, and somewhat contemptuous of the mighty men of the past. Men who are most observant as to the friends they make, or the conversation they share, are carelessness itself as to the books to whom they entrust themselves, and the printed language with which they saturate their minds. Yet can any friendship or society be more important to us than that of the books which form so large a part of our minds and even of our characters? Do we in real life take any pleasant fellow to our homes and chat with some agreeable rascal by our firesides, we who will take up any pleasant fellow's printed memoirs, we who delight in the agreeable rascal when he is cut up into pages and bound in calf?

If any person given to reading were honestly to keep a register of all the printed stuff that he or she consumes in a year—all the idle tales of which the very names and the story are forgotten in a week, the bookmaker's prattle about nothing at so much a sheet, the fugitive trifling about silly things and empty people, the memoirs of the unmemorable, and lives of those who never really lived at all—of what a mountain of rubbish would it be the catalogue: Exercises for the eye and the memory, as mechanical as if we set ourselves to learn the names, ages, and family histories of every one who lives in our own street, the flirtations of their maiden aunts, and the circumstances surrounding the birth of their grandmother's first baby.

It is impossible to give any method to our reading till we get nerve enough to reject. The most exclusive and careful amongst us will (in literature) take boon companions out of the street, as easily as an idler in a tavern. "I came across such and such a book that I never heard mentioned," says one, "and found it curious, though entirely worthless." "I strayed on a volume by I know not whom, on a subject for which I never cared." And so on. There are curious and worthless creatures enough in any pot-house all day long; and there is incessant talk in omnibus, train, or street by we know not whom, about we care not what. Yet if a printer and a bookseller can be induced to make this gabble as immortal as print and publication can make it, then it straightway is literature, and in due time it becomes "curious."

I have no intention to moralise or to indulge in a homily against the reading of what is deliberately evil. There is not so much need for this now, and I am not discoursing on the whole duty of man. I take that part of our reading which by itself is no doubt harmless, entertaining, and even gently instructive. But of this enormous mass of literature how much deserves to be chosen out, to be preferred to all the great books of the world, to be set apart for those precious hours which are all that the most of us can give to solid reading? The vast proportion of books are books that we shall never be able to read. A serious percentage of books are not worth reading at all. The really vital books for us we also know to be a very trifling portion of the whole. And yet we act as if every book were as good as any other, as if it were merely a question of order which we take up first, as if any book were good enough for us, and as if all were alike honourable, precious, and satisfying. Alas! books cannot be more than the men who write them; and as a fair proportion of the human race now write books, with motives and objects as various as human activity, books, as books, are entitled *à priori*, until their value is proved, to the same attention and respect as houses, steam-engines, pictures, fiddles, bonnets, and other products of human industry. In the shelves of those libraries which are our pride, libraries public or private, circulating or very stationary, are to be found those great books of the world *rari nantes in gurgite vasto*,[26] those books which are truly "the precious life-blood of a master-spirit." But the very familiarity which their mighty fame has bred in us makes us indifferent; we grow weary of what every one is supposed to have read; and we take down something which looks a little eccentric, some worthless book, on the mere ground that we never heard of it before.

Thus the difficulties of literature are in their way as great as those of the world, the obstacles to finding the right friends are as great, the peril is as great of being lost in a Babel of voices and an ever-changing mass of beings. Books are not wiser than men, the true books are not easier to find than the true men, the bad books or the vulgar books are not less obtrusive and not less ubiquitous than the bad or vulgar men are everywhere; the art of right reading is as long and difficult to learn as the art of right living. Those who are on good terms with the first author they meet, run as much risk as men who surrender their time to the first passer in the street; for to be open to every book is for the most part to gain as little as possible from any. A man aimlessly wandering about in a crowded city is of all men the most lonely; so he who takes up only the books that he "comes across" is pretty certain to meet but few that are worth knowing.

Now this danger is one to which we are specially exposed in this age. Our high-pressure life of emergencies, our whirling industrial organisation or disorganisation have brought us in this (as in most things) their peculiar difficulties and drawbacks. In almost everything vast opportunities and gigantic means of multiplying our products bring with them new perils and troubles which are often at first neglected. Our huge cities, where wealth is piled up and the requirements and appliances of life extended beyond the dreams of our forefathers, seem to breed in themselves new forms of squalor, disease, blights, or risks to life such as we are yet unable to master. So the enormous multiplicity of modern books is not altogether favourable to the knowing of the best. I listen with mixed satisfaction to the paeans that they chant over the works which issue from the press each day: how the books poured forth from Paternoster Row might in a few years be built into a pyramid that would fill the dome of St. Paul's. How in this mountain of literature am I to find the really useful book? How, when I have found it, and found its value, am I to get others to read it? How am I to keep my head clear in the torrent and din of works, all of which distract my attention, most of which promise me something, whilst so few fulfil that promise? The Nile is the source of the Egyptian's bread, and without it he perishes of hunger. But the Nile may be rather too liberal in his flood, and then the Egyptian runs imminent risk of drowning.

And thus there never was a time, at least during the last two hundred years, when the difficulties in the way of making an efficient use of books were greater than they are to-day, when the obstacles were more real between readers and the right books to read, when it was practically so troublesome to find out that which it is of vital importance to know; and that not by the dearth, but by the plethora of printed matter. For it comes to nearly the same thing whether we are actually debarred by physical impossibility, from getting the right book into our hand, or whether we are choked off from the right book by the obtrusive crowd of the wrong books;

so that it needs a strong character and a resolute system of reading to keep the head cool in the storm of literature around us. We read nowadays in the market-place—I would rather say in some large steam factory of letter-press, where damp sheets of new print whirl round us perpetually—if it be not rather some noisy book-fair where literary showmen tempt us with performing dolls, and the gongs of rival booths are stunning our ears from morn till night. Contrast with this pandemonium of Leipsic and Paternoster Row the sublime picture of our Milton in his early retirement at Horton, when, musing over his coming flight to the epic heaven, practising his pinions, as he tells Diodati, he consumed five years of solitude in reading the ancient writers—"*Et totum rapiunt me, mea vita, libri.*"[27]

Who now reads the ancient writers? Who systematically reads the great writers, be they ancient or modern, whom the consent of ages has marked out as classics: typical, immortal, peculiar teachers of our race? Alas! the *Paradise Lost* is lost again to us beneath an inundation of graceful academic verse, sugary stanzas of ladylike prettiness, and ceaseless explanations in more or less readable prose of what John Milton meant or did not mean, or what he saw or did not see, who married his great-aunt, and why Adam or Satan is like that, or unlike the other. We read a perfect library about the *Paradise Lost*, but the *Paradise Lost* itself we do not read.

I am not presumptuous enough to assert that the larger part of modern literature is not worth reading in itself, that the prose is not readable, entertaining, one may say highly instructive. Nor do I pretend that the verses which we read so zealously in place of Milton's are not good verses. On the contrary, I think them sweetly conceived, as musical and as graceful as the verse of any age in our history. A great deal of our modern literature is such that it is exceedingly difficult to resist it, and it is undeniable that it gives us real information. It seems perhaps unreasonable to many to assert that a decent readable book which gives us actual instruction can be otherwise than a useful companion and a solid gain. Possibly many people are ready to cry out upon me as an obscurantist for venturing to doubt a genial confidence in all literature simply as such. But the question, which weighs upon me with such really crushing urgency is this: What are the books that in our little remnant of reading time it is most vital for us to know? For the true use of books is of such sacred value to us that to be simply entertained is to cease to be taught, elevated, inspired by books; merely to gather information of a chance kind is to close the mind to knowledge of the urgent kind.

Every book that we take up without a purpose is an opportunity lost of taking up a book with a purpose—every bit of stray information which we cram into our heads without any sense of its importance, is for the most part a bit of the most useful information driven out of our heads and choked off from our minds. It is so certain that information, i.e., the knowledge, the stored thoughts and observations of mankind, is now grown to proportions so utterly incalculable and prodigious, that even the learned whose lives are given to study can but pick up some crumbs that fall from the table of truth. They delve and tend but a plot in that vast and teeming kingdom, whilst those whom active life leaves with but a few cramped hours of study can hardly come to know the very vastness of the field before them, or how infinitesimally small is the corner they can traverse at the best. We know all is not of equal value. We know that books differ in value as much as diamonds differ from the sand on the seashore, as much as our living friend differs from a dead rat. We know that much in the myriad-peopled world of books—very much in all kinds—is trivial, enervating, inane, even noxious. And thus, where we have infinite opportunities of wasting our efforts to no end, of fatiguing our minds without enriching them, of clogging the spirit without satisfying it, there, I cannot but think, the very infinity of opportunities is robbing us of the actual power of using them. And thus I come often, in my less hopeful moods, to watch the remorseless cataract of daily literature which thunders over the remnants of the past, as if it were a fresh impediment to the men of our day in the way of systematic knowledge and consistent powers of thought, as if it were destined one day to overwhelm the great inheritance of mankind in prose and verse.

I remember, when I was a very young man at college, that a youth, in no spirit of paradox, but out of plenary conviction, undertook to maintain before a body of serious students, the astounding proposition that the invention of printing had been one of the greatest misfortunes that had ever befallen mankind. He argued that exclusive reliance on printed matter had destroyed the higher method of oral teaching, the dissemination of thought by the spoken word to the attentive ear. He insisted that the formation of a vast literary class looking to the making of books as a means of making money, rather than as a social duty, had multiplied books for the sake of the writers rather than for the sake of the readers; that the reliance on books as a cheap and common resource had done much to weaken the powers of memory; that it destroyed the craving for a general culture of taste, and the need of artistic expression in all the surroundings of life. And he argued, lastly, that the sudden multiplication of all kinds of printed matter had been fatal to the orderly arrangement of thought, and had hindered a system of knowledge and a scheme of education.

I am far from sharing this immature view. Of course I hold the invention of printing to have been one of the most momentous facts in the whole history of man. Without it universal social progress, true democratic enlightenment, and the education of the people would have been impossible, or very slow, even if the cultured few, as is likely, could have advanced the knowledge of mankind without it. We place Gutenberg amongst the small list of the unique and special benefactors of mankind, in the sacred choir of those whose work transformed the conditions of life, whose work, once done, could never be repeated. And no doubt the things which our ardent friend regarded as so fatal a disturbance of society were all inevitable and necessary, part of the great revolution of mind through which men grew out of the mediaeval incompleteness to a richer conception of life and of the world.

Yet there is a sense in which this boyish anathema against printing may become true to us by our own fault. We may create for ourselves these very evils. For the art of printing has not been a gift wholly unmixed with evils; it must be used wisely if it is to be a boon to man at all; it entails on us heavy responsibilities, resolution to use it with judgment and self-control, and the will to resist its temptations and its perils. Indeed, we may easily so act that we may make it a clog on the progress of the human mind, a real curse and not a boon. The power of flying at will through space would probably extinguish civilisation and society, for it would release us from the wholesome bondage of place and rest. The power of hearing every word that had ever been uttered on this planet would annihilate thought, as the power of knowing all recorded facts by the process of turning a handle would annihilate true science. Our human faculties and our mental forces are not enlarged simply by multiplying our materials of knowledge and our facilities for communication. Telephones, microphones, pantoscopes, steam-presses, and ubiquity-engines in general may, after all, leave the poor human brain panting and throbbing under the strain of its appliances, no bigger and no stronger than the brains of the men who heard Moses speak, and saw Aristotle and Archimedes pondering over a few worn rolls of crabbed manuscript. Until some new Gutenberg or Watt can invent a machine for magnifying the human mind, every fresh apparatus for multiplying its work is a fresh strain on the mind, a new realm for it to order and to rule.

Nor will I enlarge on the matter for thought, for foreboding, almost for despair, that is presented to us by the fact of our familiar literary ways and our recognised literary profession. That things infinitely trifling in themselves: men, events, societies, phenomena, in no way otherwise more valuable than the myriad other things which flit around us like the sparrows on the housetop, should be glorified, magnified, and perpetuated, set under a literary microscope and focussed in the blaze of a literary magic-lantern—not for what they are in themselves, but solely to amuse and excite the world by showing how it can be done—all this is to me so amazing, so heart-breaking, that I forbear now to treat it, as I cannot say all that I would.

The Choice of Books is really the choice of our education, of a moral and intellectual ideal, of the whole duty of man. But though I shrink from any so high a theme, a few words are needed to indicate my general point of view in the matter.

In the first place, when we speak about books, let us avoid the extravagance of expecting too much from books, the pedant's habit of extolling books as synonymous with education. Books are no more education than laws are virtue; and just as profligacy is easy within the strict limits of law, a boundless knowledge of books may be found with a narrow education. A man may be, as the poet saith, "deep vers'd in books, and shallow in himself." We need to know in order that we may feel rightly and act wisely. The thirst after truth itself may be pushed to a degree where indulgence enfeebles our sympathies and unnerves us in action. Of all men perhaps the book-lover needs most to be reminded that man's business here is to know for the sake of living, not to live for the sake of knowing.

A healthy mode of reading would follow the lines of a sound education. And the first canon of a sound education is to make it the instrument to perfect the whole nature and character. Its aims are comprehensive, not special; they regard life as a whole, not mental curiosity; they have to give us, not so much materials, as capacities. So that, however moderate and limited the opportunity for education, in its way it should be always more or less symmetrical and balanced, appealing equally in turn to the three grand intellectual elements—imagination, memory, reflection: and so having something to give us in poetry, in history, in science, and in philosophy.

And thus our reading will be sadly one-sided, however voluminous it be, if it entirely close to us any of the great types and ideals which the creative instinct of man has produced, if it shut out from us either the ancient world, or other European poetry, as important almost as our own. When our reading, however deep, runs wholly into "pockets," and exhausts itself in the literature of one age, one country, one type, then we may be sure that it is tending to narrow or deform our minds. And the more it leads us into curious byways and nurtures us into indifference for the beaten highways of the world, the sooner we shall end, if we be not specialists and students by profession, in ceasing to treat our books as the companions and solace of our lifetime, and in using them as the instruments of a refined sort of self-indulgence.

A wise education, and so judicious reading, should leave no great type of thought, no dominant phase of human nature, wholly a blank. Whether our reading be great or small, so far as it goes, it should be general. If our lives admit of but a short space for reading, all the more reason that, so far as may be, it should remind us of the vast expanse of human thought, and the wonderful variety of human nature. To read, and yet so to read that we see nothing but a corner of literature, the loose fringe, or flats and wastes of letters, and by reading only deepen our natural belief that this island is the hub of the universe, and the nineteenth century the only age worth notice, all this is really to call in the aid of books to thicken and harden our untaught prejudices. Be it imagination, memory, or reflection that we address—that is, in poetry, history, science, or philosophy, our first duty is to aim at knowing something at least of the best, at getting some definite idea of the mighty realm whose outer rim we are permitted to approach.

But how are we to know the best; how are we to gain this definite idea of the vast world of letters? There are some who appear to suppose that the "best" are known only to experts in an esoteric way, who may reveal to inquirers what schoolboys and betting-men describe as "tips." There are no "tips" in literature; the "best" authors are never dark horses; we need no "crammers" and "coaches" to thrust us into the presence of the great writers of all time. "Crammers" will only lead us wrong. It is a thing far easier and more common than many imagine, to discover the best. It needs no research, no learning, and is only misguided by recondite information. The world has long ago closed the great assize of letters and judged the first places everywhere. In such a matter the judgment of the world, guided and informed by a long succession of accomplished critics, is almost unerring. When some Zoilus finds blemishes in Homer, and prefers, it may be, the work of some Apollonius of his own discovering, we only laugh. There may be doubts about the third and fourth rank; but the first and the second are hardly open to discussion. The gates which lead to the Elysian fields may slowly wheel back on their adamantine hinges to admit now and then some new and chosen modern. But the company of the masters of those who know, and in especial degree of the great poets, is a roll long closed and complete, and they who are of it hold ever peaceful converse together.

Hence we may find it a useful maxim that, if our reading be utterly closed to the great poems of the world, there is something amiss with our reading. If you find Milton, Dante, Calderon, Goethe, so much "Hebrew-Greek" to you; if your Homer and Virgil, your Molière and Scott, rest year after year undisturbed on their shelves beside your school trigonometry and your old college text-books; if you have never opened the *Cid, the*

Nibelungen, *Crusoe*, and *Don Quixote* since you were a boy, and are wont to leave the Bible and the Imitation for some wet Sunday afternoon—know, friend, that your reading can do you little real good. Your mental digestion is ruined or sadly out of order. No doubt, to thousands of intelligent educated men who call themselves readers, the reading through a Canto of *The Purgatorio*, or a Book of the *Paradise Lost*, is a task as irksome as it would be to decipher an ill-written manuscript in a language that is almost forgotten. But, although we are not to be always reading epics, and are chiefly in the mood for slighter things, to be absolutely unable to read Milton or Dante with enjoyment, is to be in a very bad way. Aristophanes, Theocritus, Boccaccio, Cervantes, Molière are often as light as the driven foam; but they are not light enough for the general reader. Their humour is too bright and lovely for the groundlings. They are, alas! "classics," somewhat apart from our everyday ways; they are not banal enough for us; and so for us they slumber "unknown in a long night," just *because* they are immortal poets, and are not scribblers of to-day.

When will men understand that the reading of great books is a faculty to be acquired, not a natural gift, at least not to those who are spoiled by our current education and habits of life? *Ceci tuera cela*,[28] the last great poet might have said of the first circulating library. An insatiable appetite for new novels makes it as hard to read a masterpiece as it seems to a Parisian boulevardier to live in a quiet country. Until a man can truly enjoy a draft of clear water bubbling from a mountain side, his taste is in an unwholesome state. And so he who finds the Heliconian spring insipid should look to the state of his nerves. Putting aside the iced air of the difficult mountain tops of epic, tragedy, or psalm, there are some simple pieces which may serve as an unerring test of a healthy or a vicious taste for imaginative work. If the *Cid*, the *Vita Nuova*, the *Canterbury Tales*, Shakespeare's *Sonnets*, and *Lycidas* pall on a man; if he care not for Malory's *Morte d'Arthur* and the *Red Cross Knight*; if he thinks *Crusoe* and the *Vicar* books for the young; if he thrill not with *The Ode to the West Wind,* and *The Ode to a Grecian Urn*; if he have no stomach for *Christabel* or the lines written on *The Wye above Tintern Abbey,* he should fall on his knees and pray for a cleanlier and quieter spirit.

The intellectual system of most of us in these days needs "to purge and to live cleanly." Only by a course of treatment shall we bring our minds to feel at peace with the grand pure works of the world. Something we ought all to know of the masterpieces of antiquity, and of the other nations of Europe. To understand a great national poet, such as Dante, Calderon, Corneille, or Goethe, is to know other types of human civilisation in ways which a library of histories does not sufficiently teach. The great masterpieces of the world are thus, quite apart from the charm and solace they give us, the master instruments of a solid education.

FOOTNOTES:

[Footnote 23: From "The Choice of Books," 1891. Printed here by permission of The Macmillan Company.]

[Footnote 24: Books intensely desired.]

[Footnote 25: Thing said in passing.]

[Footnote 26: Floating scattered on the vast abyss.]

[Footnote 27: "And here my books—my life—absorb me whole," Cowper's translation of Milton's Latin Epistle to Diodati.]

[Footnote 28: This will destroy that.]

ON GOING A JOURNEY[29]

WILLIAM HAZLITT

One of the pleasantest things in the world is going a journey; but I like to go by myself. I can enjoy society in a room; but out of doors, nature is company enough for me. I am then never less alone than when alone.

"The fields his study, nature was his book."

I cannot see the wit of walking and talking at the same time. When I am in the country, I wish to vegetate like the country. I am not for criticising hedge-rows and black cattle. I go out of town in order to forget the town and all that is in it. There are those who for this purpose go to watering-places, and carry the metropolis with them. I like more elbow-room, and fewer encumbrances. I like solitude, when I give myself up to it, for the sake of solitude; nor do I ask for

———"a friend in my retreat, Whom I may whisper solitude is sweet."

The soul of a journey is liberty, perfect liberty, to think, feel, do just as one pleases. We go a journey chiefly to be free of all impediments and of all inconveniences; to leave ourselves behind, much more to get rid of others.

It is because I want a little breathing-space to muse on indifferent matters, where Contemplation

"May plume her feathers and let grow her wings,
That in the various bustle of resort
Were all too ruffled, and sometimes impair'd,"

that I absent myself from the town for a while, without feeling at a loss the moment I am left by myself. Instead of a friend in a postchaise or in a Tilbury, to exchange good things with, and vary the same stale topics over again, for once let me have a truce with impertinence. Give me the clear blue sky over my head, and the green turf beneath my feet, a winding road before me, and a three hours' march to dinner—and then to thinking! It is hard if I cannot start some game on these lone heaths. I laugh, I run, I leap, I sing for joy. From the point of yonder rolling cloud, I plunge into my past being, and revel there, as the sunburnt Indian plunges headlong into the wave that wafts him to his native shore. Then long-forgotten things, like "sunken wrack and sumless treasuries," burst upon my eager sight, and I begin to feel, think, and be myself again. Instead of an awkward silence, broken by attempts at wit or dull commonplaces, mine is that undisturbed silence of the heart which alone is perfect eloquence. No one likes puns, alliterations, antitheses, arguments, and analysis better than I do; but I sometimes had rather be without them. "Leave, oh, leave me to my repose!" I have just now other business in hand, which would seem idle to you, but is with me "very stuff of the conscience." Is not this wild rose sweet without a comment? Does not this daisy leap to my heart set in its coat of emerald. Yet if I were to explain to you the circumstance that has so endeared it to me, you would only smile. Had I not better then keep it to myself, and let it serve me to brood over, from here to yonder craggy point, and from thence onward to the far-distant horizon? I should be but bad company all that way, and therefore prefer being alone. I have heard it said that you may, when the moody fit comes on, walk or ride on by yourself, and indulge your reveries. But this looks like a breach of manners, a neglect of others, and you are thinking all the time that you ought to rejoin your party. "Out upon such half-faced fellowship," say I. I like to be either entirely to myself, or entirely at the disposal of others; to talk or be silent, to walk or sit still, to be sociable or solitary. I was pleased with an observation of Mr. Cobbett's that "he thought it a bad French custom to drink our wine with our meals, and that an Englishman ought to do only one thing at a time." So I cannot talk and think, or indulge in melancholy musing and lively conversation by fits and starts. "Let me have a companion of my way," says Sterne, "were it but to remark how the shadows lengthen as the sun declines." It is beautifully said: but in my opinion, this continual comparing of notes interferes with the involuntary impression of things upon the mind, and hurts the sentiment. If you only hint what you feel in a kind of dumb show, it is insipid: if you have to explain it, it is making a toil of a pleasure. You cannot read the book of nature, without being perpetually put to the trouble of translating it for the benefit of others. I am for the synthetical method on a journey, in preference to the analytical. I am content to lay in a stock of ideas then, and to examine and anatomise them afterwards. I want to see my vague notions float like the down of the thistle before the breeze, and not to have them entangled in the briars and thorns of controversy. For once, I like to have it all my own way; and this is impossible unless you are alone, or in such company as I do not covet. I have no objection to argue a point with any one for twenty miles of measured road, but not for pleasure. If you remark the scent of a beanfield crossing the road, perhaps your fellow-traveller has no smell. If you point to a distant object, perhaps he is short-sighted, and has to take out his glass to look at it. There is a feeling in the air, a tone in the colour of a cloud which hits your fancy, but the effect of which you are unable to account for. There is then no sympathy, but an uneasy craving after it, and a dissatisfaction which pursues you on the way, and in the end probably produces ill humour. Now I never quarrel with myself, and take all my own conclusions for granted till I find it necessary to defend them against objections. It is not merely that you may not be of accord on the objects and circumstances that present themselves before you—these may recall a number of objects, and lead to associations too delicate and refined to be possibly communicated to others. Yet these I love to cherish, and sometimes still fondly clutch them, when I can escape from the throng to do so. To give way to our feelings before company, seems extravagance or affectation; and on the other hand, to have to unravel this mystery of our being at every turn, and to make others take an equal interest in it (otherwise the end is not answered) is a task to which few are competent. We must "give it an understanding, but no tongue." My old friend C——, however, could do both. He could go on in the most delightful explanatory way over hill and dale, a summer's day, and convert a landscape into a didactic poem or a Pindaric ode. "He talked far above singing." If I could so clothe my ideas in sounding and flowing words, I might perhaps wish to have some one with me to admire the swelling theme; or I could be more content, were it possible for me still to hear his echoing voice in the woods of All-Foxden. They had "that fine madness in them which our first poets had;" and if they could have been caught by some rare instrument, would have breathed such strains as the following.

   ———"Here be woods as green
 As any, air likewise as fresh and sweet
 As when smooth Zephyrus plays on the fleet
 Face of the curled stream, with flow'rs as many
 As the young spring gives, and as choice as any;
 Here be all new delights, cool streams and wells,
 Arbours o'ergrown with woodbine, caves and dells;
 Choose where thou wilt, while I sit by and sing,
 Or gather rushes to make many a ring

For thy long fingers; tell thee tales of love,
How the pale Phoebe, hunting in a grove,
First saw the boy Endymion, from whose eyes
She took eternal fire that never dies;
How she convey'd him softly in a sleep,
His temples bound with poppy, to the steep
Head of old Latmos, where she stoops each night,
Gilding the mountain with her brother's light,
To kiss her sweetest."———

FAITHFUL SHEPHERDESS.

Had I words and images at command like these, I would attempt to wake the thoughts that lie slumbering on golden ridges in the evening clouds: but at the sight of nature my fancy, poor as it is, droops and closes up its leaves, like flowers at sunset. I can make nothing out on the spot:—I must have time to collect myself.—

In general, a good thing spoils out-of-door prospects: it should be reserved for Table-talk. L—— is for this reason, I take it, the worst company in the world out of doors; because he is the best within. I grant, there is one subject on which it is pleasant to talk on a journey; and that is, what one shall have for supper when we get to our inn at night. The open air improves this sort of conversation or friendly altercation, by setting a keener edge on appetite. Every mile of the road heightens the flavour of the viands we expect at the end of it. How fine it is to enter some old town, walled and turreted, just at the approach of nightfall, or to come to some straggling village, with the lights streaming through the surrounding gloom; and then after inquiring for the best entertainment that the place affords, to "take one's ease at one's inn!" These eventful moments in our lives' history are too precious, too full of solid, heartfelt happiness to be frittered and dribbled away in imperfect sympathy. I would have them all to myself, and drain them to the last drop: they will do to talk of or to write about afterwards. What a delicate speculation it is, after drinking whole goblets of tea,

"The cups that cheer, but not inebriate,"

and letting the fumes ascend into the brain, to sit considering what we shall have for supper—eggs and a rasher, a rabbit smothered in onions, or an excellent veal-cutlet! Sancho[30] in such a situation once fixed upon cow-heel; and his choice, though he could not help it, is not to be disparaged. Then in the intervals of pictured scenery and Shandean contemplation, to catch the preparation and the stir in the kitchen—*Procul, O procul este profani!*[31] These hours are sacred to silence and to musing, to be treasured up in the memory, and to feed the source of smiling thoughts hereafter. I would not waste them in idle talk; or if I must have the integrity of fancy broken in upon, I would rather it were by a stranger than a friend. A stranger takes his hue and character from the time and place; he is a part of the furniture and costume of an inn. If he is a Quaker, or from the West Riding of Yorkshire, so much the better. I do not even try to sympathise with him, and he breaks no squares. I associate nothing with my travelling companion but present objects and passing events. In his ignorance of me and my affairs, I in a manner forget myself. But a friend reminds one of other things, rips up old grievances, and destroys the abstraction of the scene. He comes in ungraciously between us and our imaginary character. Something is dropped in the course of conversation that gives a hint of your profession and pursuits; or from having some one with you that knows the less sublime portions of your history, it seems that other people do. You are no longer a citizen of the world: but your "unhoused free condition is put into circumscription and confine." The *incognito* of an inn is one of its striking privileges—"lord of one's self, uncumber'd with a name." Oh! it is great to shake off the trammels of the world and of public opinion—to lose our importunate, tormenting, everlasting personal identity in the elements of nature, and become the creature of the moment, clear of all ties—to hold to the universe only by a dish of sweet-breads, and to owe nothing but the score of the evening—and no longer seeking for applause and meeting with contempt, to be known by no other title than *the Gentleman in the parlour*! One may take one's choice of all characters in this romantic state of uncertainty as to one's real pretensions, and become indefinitely respectable and negatively rightworshipful. We baffle prejudice and disappoint conjecture; and from being so to others, begin to be objects of curiosity and wonder even to ourselves. We are no more those hackneyed commonplaces that we appear in the world: an inn restores us to the level of nature, and quits scores with society! I have certainly spent some enviable hours at inns —sometimes when I have been left entirely to myself, and have tried to solve some metaphysical problem, as once at Witham-common, where I found out the proof that likeness is not a case of the association of ideas—at other times, when there have been pictures in the room, as at St. Neot's (I think it was) where I first met with Gribelin's engravings of the Cartoons, into which I entered at once, and at a little inn on the borders of Wales, where there happened to be hanging some of Westall's drawings, which I compared triumphantly (for a theory that I had, not for the admired artist) with the figure of a girl who had ferried me over the Severn, standing up in the boat between me and the twilight—at other times I might mention luxuriating in books, with a peculiar interest in this way, as I remember sitting up half the night to read Paul and Virginia, which I picked up at an inn at Bridgewater, after being drenched in the rain all day; and at the same place I got through two volumes of Madame D'Arblay's Camilla. It was on the tenth of April, 1798, that I sat down to a volume of the New Eloise, at the inn at Llangollen, over a bottle of sherry and a cold chicken. The letter I chose was that in which St. Preux describes his feelings as he first caught a glimpse from the heights of the Jura of the Pays de Vaud, which I had brought with me as a *bon bouche*[32], to crown the evening with. It was my birthday, and I had for the first time come from a place in the neighbourhood to visit this delightful spot. The road to Llangollen turns off between Chirk and Wrexham; and on passing a certain point, you come all at once upon the valley, which opens like an amphitheatre, broad, barren hills rising in majestic state on either side, with "green upland swells that echo to the bleat of flocks" below, and the river Dee babbling over its stony bed in the midst of them. The valley at this time "glittered green with sunny showers," and a budding ash-tree dipped its tender branches in the chiding stream. How proud, how glad I was to walk along the high road that overlooks the delicious prospect, repeating the lines which I have just quoted from Mr. Coleridge's poems! But besides the prospect which opened beneath my feet, another also opened to my inward sight, a heavenly vision, on which were written, in letters large as Hope could make them, these four words, LIBERTY, GENIUS, LOVE, VIRTUE; which have since faded into the light of common day, or mock my idle gaze.

"The beautiful is vanished, and returns not."

Still I would return some time or other to this enchanted spot; but I would return to it alone. What other self could I find to share that influx of thoughts, of regret, and delight, the fragments of which I could hardly conjure up to myself, so much have they been broken and defaced! I could stand on some tall rock, and overlook the precipice of years that separates me from what I then was. I was at that time going shortly to visit the poet whom I have above named. Where is he now? Not only I myself have changed; the world, which was then new to me, has become old and incorrigible. Yet will I turn to thee in thought, O sylvan Dee, in joy, in youth and gladness as thou then wert; and thou shalt always be to me the river of Paradise, where I will drink of the waters of life freely!

There is hardly any thing that shows the short-sightedness or capriciousness of the imagination more than travelling does. With change of place we change our ideas; nay, our opinions and feelings. We can by an effort indeed transport ourselves to old and long-forgotten scenes, and then the picture of the mind revives again; but we forget those that we have just left. It seems that we can think but of one place at a time. The canvas of the fancy is but of a certain extent, and if we paint one set of objects upon it, they immediately efface every other. We cannot enlarge our conceptions, we only shift our point of view. The landscape bares its bosom to the enraptured eye, we take our fill of it, and seem as if we could form no other image of beauty or grandeur. We pass on, and think no more of it: the horizon that shuts it from our sight, also blots it from our memory like a dream. In travelling through a wild barren country, I can form no idea of a woody and cultivated one. It appears to me that all the world must be barren, like what I see of it. In the country we forget the town, and in town we despise the country. "Beyond Hyde Park," says Sir Fopling Flutter, "all is a desert." All that part of the map that we do not see before us is a blank. The world in our conceit of it is not much bigger than a nutshell. It is not one prospect expanded into another, county joined to county, kingdom to kingdom, lands to seas, making an image voluminous and vast;—the mind can form no larger idea of space than the eye can take in at a single glance. The rest is a name written in a map, a calculation of arithmetic. For instance, what is the true signification of that immense mass of territory and population, known by the name of China, to us? An inch of paste-board on a wooden globe, of no more account than a China orange! Things near us are seen of the size of life: things at a distance are diminished to the size of the understanding. We measure the universe by ourselves, and even comprehend the texture of our own being only piecemeal. In this way, however, we remember an infinity of things and places. The mind is like a mechanical instrument that plays a great variety of tunes, but it must play them in succession. One idea recalls another, but it at the same time excludes all others. In trying to renew old recollections, we cannot as it were unfold the whole web of our existence; we must pick out the single threads. So in coming to a place where we have formerly lived and with which we have intimate associations, every one must have found that the feeling grows more vivid the nearer we approach the spot, from the mere anticipation of the actual impression: we remember circumstances, feelings, persons, faces, names, that we had not thought of for years; but for the time all the rest of the world is forgotten!

To return to the question I have quitted above. I have no objection to go to see ruins, aqueducts, pictures, in company with a friend or a party, but rather the contrary, for the former reason reversed. They are intelligible matters, and will bear talking about. The sentiment here is not tacit, but communicable and overt. Salisbury Plain is barren of criticism, but Stonehenge will bear a discussion antiquarian, picturesque, and philosophical. In setting out on a party of pleasure, the first consideration always is where we shall go to; in taking a solitary ramble, the question is what we shall meet with by the way. "The mind is its own place;" nor are we anxious to arrive at the end of our journey. I can myself do the honours indifferently well to works of art and curiosity. I once took a party to Oxford with no mean *éclat*—showed them that seat of the Muses at a distance,

"With glistering spires and pinnacles adorn'd"—

descanted on the learned air that breathes from the grassy quadrangles and stone walls of halls and colleges—was at home in the Bodleian; and at Blenheim quite superseded the powdered Ciceroni that attended us, and that pointed, in vain with his wand to commonplace beauties in matchless pictures.—As another exception to the above reasoning, I should not feel confident in venturing on a journey in a foreign country without a companion. I should want at intervals to hear the sound of my own language. There is an involuntary antipathy in the mind of an Englishman to foreign manners and notions that requires the assistance of social sympathy to carry it off. As the distance from home increases, this relief, which was at first a luxury, becomes a passion and an appetite. A person would almost feel stifled to find himself in the deserts of Arabia without friends and countrymen: there must be allowed to be something in the view of Athens or old Rome that claims the utterance of speech; and I own that the Pyramids are too mighty for any single contemplation. In such situations, so opposite to all one's ordinary train of ideas, one seems a species by one's self, a limb torn off from society, unless one can meet with instant fellowship and support.—Yet I did not feel this want or craving very pressing once, when I first set my foot on the laughing shores of France. Calais was peopled with novelty and delight. The confused, busy murmur of the place was like oil and wine poured into my ears; nor did the mariners' hymn, which was sung from the top of an old crazy vessel in the harbour, as the sun went down, send an alien sound into my soul. I only breathed the air of general humanity. I walked over "the vine-covered hills and gay regions of France," erect and satisfied; for the image of man was not cast down and chained to the foot of arbitrary thrones: I was at no loss for language, for that of all the great schools of painting was open to me. The whole is vanished like a shade. Pictures, heroes, glory, freedom, all are fled: nothing remains but the Bourbons and the French people!—There is undoubtedly a sensation in travelling into foreign parts that is to be had nowhere else: but it is more pleasing at the time than lasting. It is too remote from our habitual associations to be a common topic of discourse or reference, and, like a dream or another state of existence, does not piece into our daily modes of life. It is an animated but a momentary hallucination. It demands an effort to exchange our actual for our ideal identity; and to feel the pulse of our old transports revive very keenly, we must "jump" all our present comforts and connections. Our romantic and itinerant character is not to be domesticated. Dr. Johnson remarked how little foreign travel added to the facilities of conversation in those who had been abroad. In fact, the time we have spent there is both delightful and in one sense instructive; but it appears to be cut out of our substantial, downright existence, and never to join kindly on to it. We are not the same, but another, and perhaps more enviable individual, all the time we are out of our own country. We are lost to ourselves, as well as our friends. So the poet somewhat quaintly sings,

"Out of my country and myself I go."

Those who wish to forget painful thoughts, do well to absent themselves for a while from the ties and objects that recall them: but we can be said only to fulfil our destiny in the place that gave us birth. I should on this account like well enough to spend the whole of my life in travelling abroad, if I could any where borrow another life to spend afterwards at home!

FOOTNOTES:

[Footnote 29: From "Table-Talk," 1821-2.]

[Footnote 30: Sancho Panza, a character in Cervantes' romance, "Don Quixote."]

[Footnote 31: Aloof, O keep aloof, ye uninitiated!]

[Footnote 32: A titbit.]

THE REGRETS OF A MOUNTAINEER[33]

LESLIE STEPHEN

I have often felt a sympathy, which almost rises to the pathetic, when looking on at a cricket-match or boat-race. Something of the emotion with which Gray regarded the "distant spires and antique towers" rises within me. It is not, indeed, that I feel very deeply for the fine ingenuous lads who, as somebody says, are about to be degraded into tricky, selfish Members of Parliament. I have seen too much of them. They are very fine animals; but they are rather too exclusively animal. The soul is apt to be in too embryonic a state within these cases of well-strung bone and muscle. It is impossible for a mere athletic machine, however finely constructed, to appeal very deeply to one's finer sentiments. I can scarcely look forward with even an affectation of sorrow for the time when, if more sophisticated, it will at least have made a nearer approach to the dignity of an intellectual being. It is not the boys who make me feel a touch of sadness; their approaching elevation to the dignity of manhood will raise them on the whole in the scale of humanity; it is the older spectators whose aspect has in it something affecting. The shaky old gentleman, who played in the days when it was decidedly less dangerous to stand up to bowling than to a cannon-ball, and who now hobbles about on rheumatic joints, by the help of a stick; the corpulent elder, who rowed when boats had gangways down their middle, and did not require as delicate a balance as an acrobat's at the top of a living pyramid—these are the persons whom I cannot see without an occasional sigh. They are really conscious that they have lost something which they can never regain; or, if they momentarily forget it, it is even more forcibly impressed upon the spectators. To see a respectable old gentleman of sixty, weighing some fifteen stone, suddenly forget a third of his weight and two-thirds of his years, and attempt to caper like a boy, is indeed a startling phenomenon. To the thoughtless, it may be simply comic; but, without being a Jaques, one may contrive also to suck some melancholy out of it.

Now, as I have never caught a cricket-ball, and, on the contrary, have caught numerous crabs in my life, the sympathy which I feel for these declining athletes is not due to any great personal interest in the matter. But I have long anticipated that a similar day would come for me, when I should no longer be able to pursue my favourite sport of mountaineering. Some day I should find that the ascent of a zigzag was as bad as a performance on the treadmill; that I could not look over a precipice without a swimming in the head; and that I could no more jump a crevasse than the Thames at Westminster. None of these things have come to pass. So far as I know, my physical powers are still equal to the ascent of Mont Blanc or the Jungfrau. But I am no less effectually debarred—it matters not how—from mountaineering. I wander at the foot of the gigantic Alps, and look up longingly to the summits, which are apparently so near, and yet know that they are divided from me by an impassable gulf. In some missionary work I have read that certain South Sea Islanders believed in a future paradise where the good should go on eating for ever with insatiable appetites at an inexhaustible banquet. They were to continue their eternal dinner in a house with open wickerwork sides; and it was to be the punishment of the damned to crawl outside in perpetual hunger and look in through the chinks as little boys look in through the windows of a London cookshop. With similar feelings I lately watched through a telescope the small black dots, which were really men, creeping up the high flanks of Mont Blanc or Monte Rosa. The eternal snows represented for me the Elysian fields, into which entrance was sternly forbidden, and I lingered about the spot with a mixture of pleasure and pain, in the envious contemplation of my more fortunate companions.

I know there are those who will receive these assertions with civil incredulity. Some persons assume that every pleasure with which they cannot sympathise is necessarily affectation, and hold, as a particular case of that doctrine, that Alpine travellers risk their lives merely from fashion or desire of notoriety. Others are kind enough to admit that there is something genuine in the passion, but put it on a level with the passion for climbing greased poles. They think it derogatory to the due dignity of Mont Blanc that he should be used as a greased pole, and assure us that the true pleasures of the Alps are those which are within reach of the old and the invalids, who can only creep about villages and along high-roads. I cannot well argue with such detractors from what I consider a noble sport. As for the first class, it is reduced almost to a question of veracity. I say that I enjoy being on the top of a mountain, or, indeed, halfway up a mountain; that climbing is a pleasure to me, and would be so if no one else climbed and no one ever heard of my climbing. They reply that they don't believe it. No more argument is possible than if I were to say that I liked eating olives, and some one asserted that I really eat them only out of affectation. My reply would be simply to go on eating olives; and I hope the reply of mountaineers will be to go on climbing Alps. The other assault is more intelligible. Our critics admit that we have a pleasure; but assert that it is a puerile pleasure—that it leads to an irreverent view of mountain beauty, and to oversight of that which should really most impress a refined and noble mind. To this I shall only make such an indirect reply as may result from a frank confession of my own regrets at giving up the climbing business— perhaps for ever. I am sinking, so to speak, from the butterfly to the caterpillar stage, and, if the creeping thing is really the highest of the two, it will appear that there is something in the substance of my lamentations unworthy of an intellectual being. Let me try. By way of preface, however, I admit that mountaineering, in my sense of the word, is a sport. It is a sport which, like fishing or shooting, brings one into contact with the sublimest aspects of nature; and, without setting their enjoyment before one as an ultimate end or aim, helps one indirectly to absorb and be penetrated by their influence. Still it is strictly a sport—as strictly as cricket, or rowing, or knurr and spell—and I have no wish to place it on a different footing. The game is won when a mountain-top is reached in spite of difficulties; it is lost when one is forced to retreat; and, whether won or lost, it calls into play a great variety of physical and intellectual energies, and gives the pleasure which always accompanies an energetic use of our faculties. Still it suffers in some degree from this undeniable characteristic, and especially from the tinge which has consequently been communicated to narratives of mountain adventures. There are two ways which have been appropriated to the description of all sporting exploits. One is to indulge in fine writing about them, to burst out in sentences which swell to paragraphs, and in paragraphs which spread over pages; to plunge into ecstasies about infinite abysses and overpowering splendours, to compare mountains to archangels lying down in eternal winding-sheets of snow, and to convert them into allegories about man's highest destinies and aspirations. This is good when it is well done. Mr. Ruskin has covered the Matterhorn, for example, with a whole web of poetical associations, in language which, to a severe taste, is perhaps a trifle too fine, though he has done it with an eloquence which his bitterest antagonists must freely acknowledge. Yet most humble writers will feel that if they try to imitate Mr. Ruskin's eloquence they will pay the penalty of becoming ridiculous. It is not every one who can with impunity compare Alps to archangels. Tall talk is luckily an object of suspicion to Englishmen, and consequently most writers, and especially those who frankly adopt the sporting view of the mountains, adopt the opposite scheme: they affect something like cynicism; they mix descriptions of scenery with allusions to fleas or to bitter beer; they shrink with the prevailing dread of Englishmen from the danger of overstepping the limits of the sublime into its proverbial opposite; and they humbly try to amuse us because they can't strike us with awe. This, too, if I may venture to say so, is good in its way and place; and it seems rather hard to these luckless writers when people assume that, because they make jokes on a mountain, they are necessarily insensible to its awful sublimities. A sense of humour is not incompatible with imaginative sensibility; and even Wordsworth might have been an equally powerful prophet of nature if he could sometimes have descended from his stilts. In short, a man may worship mountains, and yet have a quiet joke with them when he is wandering all day in their tremendous solitudes.

Joking, however, is, it must be admitted, a dangerous habit. I freely avow that, in my humble contributions to Alpine literature, I have myself made some very poor and very unseasonable witticisms. I confess my error, and only wish that I had no worse errors to confess. Still I think that the poor little jokes in which we mountaineers sometimes indulge have been made liable to rather harsh constructions. We are accused, in downright earnest, not merely of being flippant, but of an arrogant contempt for all persons whose legs are not as strong as our own. We are supposed seriously to wrap ourselves in our own conceit, and to brag intolerably of our exploits. Now I will not say that no mountaineer ever swaggers: the quality called by the vulgar "bounce" is unluckily confined to no profession. Certainly I have seen a man intolerably vain because he could raise a hundred-weight with his little finger; and I dare say that the "champion bill-poster," whose name is advertised on the walls of this metropolis, thinks excellence in bill-posting the highest virtue of a citizen. So some men may be silly enough to brag in all seriousness about mountain exploits. However, most lads of twenty learn that it is silly to give themselves airs about mere muscular eminence; and especially is this true of Alpine exploits—first, because they require less physical prowess than almost any other sport, and secondly, because a good amateur still feels himself the hopeless inferior of half the Alpine peasants whom he sees. You cannot be very conceited about a game in which the first clodhopper you meet can give you ten minutes' start in an hour. Still a man writing in a humorous vein naturally adopts a certain bumptious tone, just as our friend "Punch" ostentatiously declares himself to be omniscient and infallible. Nobody takes him at his word, or supposes that the editor of "Punch" is really the most conceited man in all England. But we poor mountaineers are occasionally fixed with our own careless talk by some outsider who is not in the secret. We know ourselves to be a small sect, and to be often laughed at; we reply by: assuming that we are the salt of the earth, and that our amusement is the first and noblest of all amusements. Our only retort to the good-humoured ridicule with which we are occasionally treated is to adopt an affected strut, and to carry it off as if we were the finest fellows in the world. We make a boast of our shame, and say, if you laugh we must crow. But we don't really mean anything: if we did, the only word which the English language would afford wherewith to describe us would be the very unpleasant antithesis to wise men, and certainly I hold that we have the average amount of common sense. When, therefore, I see us taken to task for swaggering, I think it a trifle hard that this merely playful affectation of superiority should be made a serious fault. For the future I would promise to be careful, if it were worth avoiding the misunderstanding of men who won't take a joke. Meanwhile, I can only state that when Alpine travellers indulge in a little swagger about their own performances and other people's incapacity, they don't mean more than an infinitesimal fraction of what they say, and that they know perfectly well that when history comes to pronounce a final judgment upon the men of the time, it won't put mountain-climbing on a level with patriotism, or even with excellence in the fine arts.

The reproach of real *bonâ fide* arrogance is, so far as I know, very little true of Alpine travellers. With the exception of the necessary fringe hanging on to every set of human beings—consisting of persons whose heads are weaker than their legs—the mountaineer, so far as my experience has gone, is generally modest enough. Perhaps he sometimes flaunts his ice-axes and ropes a little too much before the public eye at Chamonix, as a yachtsman occasionally flourishes his nautical costume at Cowes; but the fault may be pardoned by those not inexorable to human weaknesses. This opinion, I know, cuts at the root of the most popular theory as to our ruling passion. If we do not climb the Alps to gain notoriety, for what purpose can we possibly climb them? That same unlucky trick of joking is taken to indicate that we don't care much about the scenery; for who, with a really susceptible soul, could be facetious under the cliffs of Jungfrau or the ghastly precipices of the Matterhorn? Hence people who kindly excuse us from the blame of notoriety-hunting generally accept the "greased-pole" theory. We are, it seems, overgrown schoolboys, who, like other schoolboys, enjoy being in dirt, and danger, and mischief, and have as much sensibility for natural beauty as the mountain mules. And against this, as a more serious complaint, I wish to make my feeble protest, in order that my lamentations on quitting the profession may not seem unworthy of a thinking being.

Let me try to recall some of the impressions which mountaineering has left with me, and see whether they throw any light upon the subject. As I gaze at the huge cliffs where I may no longer wander, I find innumerable recollections arise—some of them dim, as though belonging to a past existence; and some so brilliant that I can scarcely realise my exclusion from the scenes to which they belong. I am standing at the foot of what, to my mind, is the most glorious of all Alpine wonders—the huge Oberland precipice, on the slopes of the Faulhorn or the Wengern Alp. Innumerable tourists have done all that tourists can do to cocknify (if that is the right derivative from cockney) the scenery; but, like the Pyramids or a Gothic cathedral, it throws off the taint of vulgarity by its imperishable majesty. Even on turf strewn with sandwich-papers and empty bottles, even in the presence of hideous peasant-women singing "Stand-er auf" for five centimes, we cannot but feel the influence of Alpine beauty. When the sunlight is dying off the snows, or the full moon lighting them up with ethereal tints, even sandwich-papers and singing women may be forgotten. How does the memory of scrambles along snow arêtes, of plunges—luckily not too deep—into crevasses, of toil through long snowfields, towards a refuge that seemed to recede as we advanced—where, to quote Tennyson with due alteration, to the traveller toiling in immeasurable snow—

> Sown in a wrinkle of the monstrous hill
> The châlet sparkles like a grain of salt;—

how do such memories as these harmonise with the sense of superlative sublimity?

One element of mountain beauty is, we shall all admit, their vast size and steepness. That a mountain is very big, and is faced by perpendicular walls of rock, is the first thing which strikes everybody, and is the whole essence and outcome of a vast quantity of poetical description. Hence the first condition towards a due appreciation of mountain scenery is that these qualities should be impressed upon the imagination. The mere dry statement that a mountain is so many feet in vertical height above the sea, and contains so many tons of granite, is nothing. Mont Blanc, is about three miles high. What of that? Three miles is an hour's walk for a lady—an eighteen-penny cab-fare—the distance from Hyde Park Corner to the Bank—an express train could do it in three minutes, or a racehorse in five. It is a measure which we have learnt to despise, looking at it from a horizontal point of view; and accordingly most persons, on seeing the Alps for the first time, guess them to be higher, as measured in feet, than they really are. What, indeed, is the use of giving measures in feet to any but the scientific mind? Who cares whether the moon is 250,000 or 2,500,000 miles distant? Mathematicians try to impress upon us that the distance of the fixed stars is only expressible by a row of figures which stretches across a page; suppose it stretched across two or across a dozen pages, should we be any the wiser, or have, in the least degree, a clearer notion of the superlative distances? We civilly say, "Dear me!" when the astronomer looks to us for the appropriate stare, but we only say it with the mouth; internally our remark is, "You might as well have multiplied by a few more millions whilst you were about it." Even astronomers, though not a specially imaginative race, feel the impotence of figures, and try to give us some measure which the mind can grasp a little more conveniently. They tell us about the cannon-ball which might have been flying ever since the time of Adam, and not yet have reached the heavenly body, or about the stars which may not yet have become visible, though the light has been flying to us at a rate inconceivable by the mind for an inconceivable number of years; and they succeed in producing a bewildering and giddy sensation, although the numbers are too vast to admit of any accurate apprehension.

We feel a similar need in the case of mountains. Besides the bare statement of figures, it is necessary to have some means for grasping the meaning of the figures. The bare tens and thousands must be clothed with some concrete images. The statement that a mountain is 15,000 feet high is, by itself, little more impressive, than that it is 3,000; we want something more before we can mentally compare Mont Blanc and Snowdon. Indeed, the same people who guess of a mountain's height at a number of feet much exceeding the reality, show, when they are cross-examined, that they fail to appreciate in any tolerable degree the real meaning of the figures. An old lady one day, about 11 A.M., proposed to walk from the Aeggischhorn to the Jungfrau-Joch, and to return for luncheon—the distance being a good twelve hours' journey for trained mountaineers. Every detail of which the huge mass is composed is certain to be underestimated. A gentleman the other day pointed out to me a grand ice-cliff at the end of a hanging glacier, which must have been at least 100 feet high, and asked me whether that snow was three feet deep. Nothing is more common than for tourists to mistake some huge pinnacle of rock, as big as a church tower, for a traveller. The rocks of the Grands Mulets, in one corner of which the châlet is hidden, are often identified with a party ascending Mont Blanc; and I have seen boulders as big as a house pointed out confidently as chamois. People who make these blunders must evidently see the mountains as mere toys, however many feet they may give them at a random guess. Huge overhanging cliffs are to them steps within the reach of human legs; yawning crevasses are ditches to be jumped; and foaming waterfalls are like streams from penny squirts. Everyone knows the avalanches on the Jungfrau, and the curiously disproportionate appearance of the little puffs of white smoke, which are said to be the cause of the thunder; but the disproportion ceases to an eye that has learnt really to measure distance, and to know that these smoke-puffs, represent a cataract of crashing blocks of ice.

Now the first merit of mountaineering is that it enables one to have what theologians would call an experimental faith in the size of mountains—to substitute a real living belief for a dead intellectual assent. It enables one, first, to assign something like its true magnitude to a rock or snow-slope; and, secondly, to measure that magnitude in terms of muscular exertion instead of bare mathematical units. Suppose that we are standing upon the Wengern Alp; between the Mönch and the Eiger there stretches a round white bank, with a curved outline, which we may roughly compare to the back of one of Sir E. Landseer's lions. The ordinary tourists—the old man, the woman, or the cripple, who are supposed to appreciate the real beauties of Alpine scenery—may look at it comfortably from their hotel. They may see its graceful curve, the long straight lines that are ruled in delicate shading down its sides, and the contrast of the blinding white snow with the dark blue sky above; but they will probably guess it to be a mere bank—a snowdrift, perhaps, which has been piled by the last storm. If you pointed out to them one of the great rocky teeth that projected from its summit, and said that it was a guide, they would probably remark that he looked very small, and would fancy that he could jump over the bank with an effort. Now a mountaineer knows, to begin with, that it is a massive rocky rib, covered with snow, lying at a sharp angle, and varying perhaps from 500 to 1,000 feet in height. So far he might be accompanied by men of less soaring ambition; by an engineer who had been mapping the country, or an artist who had been carefully observing the mountains from their bases. They might learn in time to interpret correctly the real meaning of shapes at which the uninitiated guess at random. But the mountaineer can go a step further, and it is the next step which gives the real significance to those delicate curves and lines. He can translate the 500 or 1,000 feet of snow-slope into a more tangible unit of measurement. To him, perhaps, they recall the memory of a toilsome ascent, the sun beating on his head for five or six hours, the snow returning the glare with still more parching effect; a stalwart guide toiling all the weary time, cutting steps in hard blue ice, the fragments hissing and spinning down the long straight grooves in the frozen snow till they lost themselves in the yawning chasm below; and step after step taken along the slippery staircase, till at length he triumphantly sprang upon the summit of the tremendous wall that no human foot had scaled before. The little black knobs that rise above the edge represent for him huge impassable rocks, sinking on one side in scarped slippery surfaces towards the snow-field, and on the other stooping in one tremendous cliff to a distorted glacier thousands of feet below. The faint blue line across the upper névé, scarcely distinguishable to the eye, represents to one observer nothing but a trifling undulation; a second, perhaps, knows that it means a crevasse; the mountaineer remembers that it is the top of a huge chasm, thirty feet across, and perhaps ten times as deep, with perpendicular sides of glimmering blue ice, and fringed by thick rows of enormous pendent icicles. The marks that are scored in delicate lines, such as might be ruled by a diamond on glass, have been cut by innumerable streams trickling in hot weather from the everlasting snow, or ploughed by succeeding avalanches that have slipped from the huge upper snowfields above. In short, there is no insignificant line or mark that has not its memory or its indication of the strange phenomena of the upper world. True, the same picture is painted upon the retina of all classes of observers; and so Porson and a schoolboy and a peasant might receive the same physical impression from a set of black and white marks on the page of a Greek play; but to one they would be an incoherent conglomeration of unmeaning and capricious lines, to another they would represent certain sounds more or less corresponding to some English words; whilst to the scholar they would reveal some of the noblest poetry in the world, and all the associations of successful intellectual labour. I do not say that the difference is quite so great in the case of the mountains; still I am certain that no one can decipher the natural writing on the face of a snow-slope or a precipice who has not wandered amongst their recesses, and learnt by slow experience what is indicated by marks which an ignorant observer would scarcely notice. True, even one who sees a mountain for the first time may know that, as a matter of fact, a scar on the face of a cliff means, for example, a recent fall of a rock; but between the bare knowledge and the acquaintance with all which that knowledge implies—the thunder of the fall, the crash of the smaller fragments, the bounding energy of the descending mass—there is almost as much difference as between hearing that a battle has been fought and being present at it yourself. We have all read descriptions of Waterloo till we are sick of the subject; but I imagine that our emotions on seeing the shattered well of Hougomont are very inferior to those of one of the Guard who should revisit the place where he held out for a long day against the assaults of the French army.

Now to an old mountaineer the Oberland cliffs are full of memories; and, more than this, he has learnt the language spoken by every crag and every wave of glacier. It is strange if they do not affect him rather more powerfully than the casual visitor who has never been initiated by practical experience into their difficulties. To him, the huge buttress which runs down from the Mönch is something more than an irregular pyramid, purple with white patches at the bottom and pure white at the top. He fills up the bare outline supplied by the senses with a thousand lively images. He sees tier above tier of rock, rising in a gradually ascending scale of difficulty, covered at first by long lines of the débris that have been splintered by frost from the higher wall, and afterwards rising bare and black and threatening. He knows instinctively which of the ledges has a dangerous look—where such a bold mountaineer as John Lauener might slip on the polished surface, or be in danger of an avalanche from above. He sees the little shell-like swelling at the foot of the glacier crawling down the steep slope above, and knows that it means an almost inaccessible wall of ice; and the steep snowfields that rise towards the summit are suggestive of something very different from the picture which might have existed in the mind of a German student, who once asked me whether it was possible to make the ascent on a mule.

Hence, if mountains owe their influence upon the imagination in a great degree to their size and steepness, and apparent inaccessibility—as no one can doubt that they do, whatever may be the explanation of the fact that people like to look at big, steep, inaccessible objects—the advantages of the mountaineer are obvious. He can measure those qualities on a very different scale from the ordinary traveler. He measures the size, not by the vague abstract term of so many thousand feet, but by the hours of labour, divided into minutes—each separately felt—of strenuous muscular exertion. The steepness is not expressed in degrees, but by the memory of the sensation produced when a snow-slope seems to be rising up and smiting you in the face; when, far away from all human help, you are clinging like a fly to the slippery side of a mighty pinnacle in mid air. And as for the inaccessibility, no one can measure the difficulty of climbing a hill who has not wearied his muscles and brain in struggling against the opposing obstacles. Alpine travellers, it is said, have removed the romance from the mountains by climbing them. What they have really done is to prove that there exists a narrow line by which a way may be found to the top of any given mountain; but the clue leads through innumerable inaccessibilities; true, you can follow one path, but to right and left are cliffs which no human foot will ever tread, and whose terrors can only be realised when you are in their immediate neighbourhood. The cliffs of the Matterhorn do not bar the way to the top effectually, but it is only by forcing a passage through them that you can really appreciate their terrible significance.

Hence I say that the qualities which strike every sensitive observer are impressed upon the mountaineer with tenfold force and intensity. If he is as accessible to poetical influences as his neighbours—and I don't know why he should be less so—he has opened new avenues of access between the scenery and his mind. He has learnt a language which is but partially revealed to ordinary men. An artist is superior to an unlearned picture-seer, not merely because he has greater natural sensibility, but because he has improved it by methodical experience; because his senses have been sharpened by constant practice, till he can catch finer shades of colouring, and more delicate inflexions of line; because, also, the lines and colours have acquired new significance, and been associated with a thousand thoughts with which the mass of mankind has never cared to connect them. The mountaineer is improved by a similar process. But I know some sceptical critics will ask, does not the way in which he is accustomed to regard mountains rather deaden their poetical influence? Doesn't he come to look at them as mere instruments of sport, and overlook their more spiritual teaching? Does not all the excitement of personal adventure and the noisy apparatus of guides, and ropes, and axes, and tobacco, and the fun of climbing, rather dull his perceptions and incapacitate him from perceiving

>   The silence that is in the starry sky,
> The sleep that is among the lonely hills?

Well, I have known some stupid and unpoetical mountaineers; and, since I have been dismounted from my favourite hobby, I think I have met some similar specimens among the humbler class of tourists. There are persons, I fancy, who "do" the Alps; who look upon the Lake of Lucerne as one more task ticked off from their memorandum book, and count up the list of summits visible from the Görnergrat without being penetrated with any keen sense of sublimity. And there are mountaineers who are capable of making a pun on the top of Mont Blanc—and capable of nothing more. Still I venture to deny that even punning is incompatible with poetry, or that those who make the pun can have no deeper feeling in their bosoms which they are perhaps too shamefaced to utter.

The fact is that that which gives its inexpressible charm to mountaineering is the incessant series of exquisite natural scenes, which are for the most part enjoyed by the mountaineer alone. This is, I am aware, a round assertion; but I will try to support it by a few of the visions which are recalled to me by these Oberland cliffs, and which I have seen profoundly enjoyed by men who perhaps never mentioned them again, and probably in describing their adventures scrupulously avoided the danger of being sentimental.

Thus every traveller has occasionally done a sunrise, and a more lamentable proceeding than the ordinary view of a sunrise can hardly be imagined. You are cold, miserable, breakfastless; have risen shivering from a warm bed, and in your heart long only to creep into bed again. To the mountaineer all this is changed. He is beginning a day full of the anticipation of a pleasant excitement. He has, perhaps, been waiting anxiously for fine weather, to try conclusions with some huge giant not yet scaled. He moves out with something of the feeling with which a soldier goes to the assault of a fortress, but without the same probability of coming home in fragments; the danger is trifling enough to be merely exhilatory, and to give a pleasant tension to the nerves; his muscles feel firm and springy, and his stomach—no small advantage to the enjoyment of scenery—is in excellent order. He looks at the sparkling stars with keen satisfaction, prepared to enjoy a fine sunrise with all his faculties at their best, and with the added pleasure of a good omen for his day's work. Then a huge dark mass begins to mould itself slowly out of the darkness, the sky begins to form a background of deep purple, against which the outline becomes gradually more definite; one by one, the peaks catch the exquisite Alpine glow, lighting up in rapid succession, like a vast illumination; and when at last the steady sunlight settles upon them, and shows every rock and glacier, without even a delicate film of mist to obscure them, he feels his heart bound, and steps out gaily to the assault—just as the people on the Rigi are giving thanks that the show is over and that they may go to bed. Still grander is the sight when the mountaineer has already reached some lofty ridge, and, as the sun rises, stands between the day and the night—the valley still in deep sleep, with the mists lying between the folds of the hills, and the snow-peaks standing out clear and pale white just before the sun reaches them, whilst a broad band of orange light runs all round the vast horizon. The glory of sunsets is equally increased in the thin upper air. The grandest of all such sights that live in my memory is that of a sunset from the Aiguille du Goûté. The snow at our feet was glowing with rich light, and the shadows in our footsteps a vivid green by the contrast. Beneath us was a vast horizontal floor of thin level mists suspended in mid air, spread like a canopy over the whole boundless landscape, and tinged with every hue of sunset. Through its rents and gaps we could see the lower mountains, the distant plains, and a fragment of the Lake of Geneva lying in a more sober purple. Above us rose the solemn mass of Mont Blanc in the richest glow of an Alpine sunset. The sense of lonely sublimity was almost oppressive, and although half our party was suffering from sickness, I believe even the guides were moved to a sense of solemn beauty.

These grand scenic effects are occasionally seen by ordinary travellers, though the ordinary traveller is for the most part out of temper at 3 A.M. The mountaineer can enjoy them, both because his frame of mind is properly trained to receive the natural beauty, and because he alone sees them with their best accessories, amidst the silence of the eternal snow, and the vast panoramas visible from the loftier summits. And he has a similar advantage in most of the great natural phenomena of the cloud and the sunshine. No sight in the Alps is more impressive than the huge rocks of a black precipice suddenly frowning out through the chasms of a storm-cloud. But grand as such a sight may be from the safe verandahs of the inn at Grindelwald, it is far grander in the silence of the Central Alps amongst the savage wilderness of rock and snow. Another characteristic effect of the High Alps often presents itself when one has been climbing for two or three hours, with nothing in sight but the varying wreaths of mist that chased each other monotonously along the rocky ribs up whose snow-covered backbone we were laboriously fighting our way. Suddenly there is a puff of wind, and looking round we find that we have in an instant pierced the clouds, and emerged, as it were, on the surface of the ocean of vapour. Beneath us stretches for hundreds of miles the level fleecy floor, and above us shines out clear in the eternal sunshine every mountain, from Mont Blanc to Monte Rosa and the Jungfrau. What, again, in the lower regions, can equal the mysterious charm of gazing from the edge of a torn rocky parapet into an apparently fathomless abyss, where nothing but what an Alpine traveller calls a "strange formless wreathing of vapour" indicates the storm-wind that is raging below us? I might go on indefinitely recalling the strangely impressive scenes that frequently startle the traveller in the waste upper world; but language is feeble indeed to convey even a glimmering of what is to be seen to those who have not seen it for themselves, whilst to them it can be little more than a peg upon which to hang their own recollections. These glories, in which the mountain Spirit reveals himself to his true worshippers, are only to be gained by the appropriate service of climbing—at some risk, though a very trifling risk, if he is approached with due form and ceremony—into the furthest recesses of his shrines. And without seeing them, I maintain that no man has really seen the Alps.

The difference between the exoteric and the esoteric school of mountaineers may be indicated by their different view of glaciers. At Grindelwald, for example, it is the fashion to go and "see the glaciers"—heaven save the mark! Ladies in costumes, heavy German professors, Americans doing the Alps at a gallop, Cook's tourists, and other varieties of a well-known genus, go off in shoals and see—what? A gigantic mass of ice, strangely torn with a few of the exquisite blue crevasses, but denied and prostrate in dirt and ruins. A stream foul with mud oozes out from the base; the whole mass seems to be melting fast away; the summer sun has evidently got the best of it in these lower regions, and nothing can resist him but the great mounds of decaying rock that strew the surface in confused lumps. It is as much like the glacier of the upper regions as the melting fragments of snow in a London street are like the surface of the fresh snow that has just fallen in a country field. And by way of improving its attractions a perpetual picnic is going on, and the ingenious natives have hewed a tunnel into the ice, for admission to which they charge certain centimes. The unlucky glacier reminds me at his latter end of a wretched whale stranded on a beach, dissolving into masses of blubber, and hacked by remorseless fishermen, instead of plunging at his ease in the deep blue water. Far above, where the glacier begins his course, he is seen only by the true mountaineer. There are vast amphitheatres of pure snow, of which the glacier known to tourists is merely the insignificant drainage, but whose very existence they do not generally suspect. They are utterly ignorant that from the top of the icefall which they visit you may walk for hours on the eternal ice. After a long climb you come to the region where the glacier is truly at its noblest; where the surface is a spotless white; where the crevasses are enormous rents sinking to profound depths, with walls of the purest blue; where the glacier is torn and shattered by the energetic forces which mould it, but has an expression of superabundant power, like a full stream fretting against its banks and plunging through the vast gorges that it has hewn for itself in the course of centuries. The bases of the mountains are immersed in a deluge of cockneyism—fortunately a shallow deluge—whilst their summits rise high into the bracing air, where everything is pure and poetical.

The difference which I have thus endeavoured to indicate is more or less traceable in a wider sense. The mountains are exquisitely beautiful, indeed, from whatever points of view we contemplate them; and the mountaineer would lose much if he never saw the beauties of the lower valleys, of pasturages deep in flowers, and dark pine-forests with the summits shining from far off between the stems. Only, as it seems to me, he has the exclusive prerogative of thoroughly enjoying one—and that the most characteristic, though by no means only, element of the scenery. There may be a very good dinner spread before twenty people; but if nineteen of them were teetotalers, and the twentieth drank his wine like a man, he would be the only one to do it full justice; the others might praise the meat or the fruits, but he would alone enjoy the champagne; and in the great feast which Nature spreads before us (a stock metaphor, which emboldens me to make the comparison), the high mountain scenery acts the part of the champagne. Unluckily, too, the teetotalers are very apt, in this case also, to sit in judgment upon their more adventurous neighbours. Especially are they pleased to carp at the views from high summits. I have been constantly asked, with a covert sneer, "Did it repay you?"—a question which involves the assumption that one wants to be repaid, as though the labour were not itself part of the pleasure, and which implies a doubt that the view is really enjoyable. People are always demonstrating that the lower views are the most beautiful; and at the same time complaining that mountaineers frequently turn back without looking at the view from the top, as though that would necessarily imply that they cared nothing for scenery. In opposition to which I must first remark that, as a rule, every step of an ascent has a beauty of its own, which one is quietly absorbing even when one is not directly making it a subject of contemplation, and that the view from the top is generally the crowning glory of the whole.

It will be enough if I conclude with an attempt to illustrate this last assertion: and I will do it by still referring to the Oberland. Every visitor with a soul for the beautiful admires the noble form of the Wetterhorn—the lofty snow-crowned pyramid rising in such light and yet massive lines from its huge basement of perpendicular cliffs. The Wetterhorn has, however, a further merit. To my mind—and I believe most connoisseurs of mountain tops agree with me—it is one of the most impressive summits in the Alps. It is not a sharp pinnacle like the Weisshorn, or a cupola like Mont Blanc, or a grand rocky tooth like the Monte Rosa, but a long and nearly horizontal knife-edge, which, as seen from either end, has of course the appearance of a sharp-pointed cone. It is when balanced upon this ridge—sitting astride of the knife-edge on which one can hardly stand without giddiness—that one fully appreciates an Alpine precipice. Mr. Justice Wills has admirably described the first ascent, and the impression it made upon him, in a paper which has become classical for succeeding adventurers. Behind you the snow-slope sinks with perilous steepness towards the wilderness of glacier and rock through which the ascent has lain. But in front the ice sinks with even greater steepness for a few feet or yards. Then it curves over and disappears, and the next thing that the eye catches is the meadowland of Grindelwald, some 9,000 feet below. I have looked down many precipices, where the eye can trace the course of every pebble that bounds down the awful slopes, and where I have shuddered as some dislodged fragment of rock showed the course which, in case of accident, fragments of my own body would follow. A precipice is always, for obvious reasons, far more terrible from above than from below. The creeping, tingling sensation which passes through one's limbs—even when one knows oneself to be in perfect safety—testifies to the thrilling influence of the sight. But I have never so realised the terrors of a terrific cliff as when I could not see it. The awful gulf which intervened between me and the green meadows struck the imagination by its invisibility. It was like the view which may be seen from the ridge of a cathedral roof, where the eaves have for their immediate background the pavement of the streets below; only this cathedral was 9,000 feet high. Now, any one standing at the foot of the Wetterhorn may admire their stupendous massiveness and steepness; but, to feel their influence enter in the very marrow of one's bones, it is necessary to stand at the summit, and to fancy the one little slide down the short ice-slope, to be followed apparently by a bound into clear air and a fall down to the houses, from heights where only the eagle ventures to soar.

This is one of the Alpine beauties, which, of course, is: beyond the power of art to imitate, and which people are therefore apt to ignore. But it is not the only one to be seen on the high summits. It is often said that these views are not "beautiful"—apparently because they won't go into a picture, or, to put it more fairly, because no picture: can in the faintest degree imitate them. But without quarrelling about words, I think that, even if "beautiful" be not the most correct epithet, they have a marvellously stimulating effect upon the imagination. Let us look round from this wonderful pinnacle in mid air, and note one or two of the most striking elements of the scenery.

You are, in the first place, perched on a cliff, whose presence is the more felt because it is unseen. Then you are in a region over which eternal silence is brooding. Not a sound ever comes there, except the occasional fall of a splintered fragment of rock, or a layer of snow; no stream is heard trickling, and the sounds of animal life are left thousands of feet below. The most that you can hear is some mysterious noise made by the wind eddying round the gigantic rocks; sometimes a strange flapping sound, as if an unearthly flag were shaking its invisible folds in the air. The enormous tract of country over which your view extends—most of it dim and almost dissolved into air by distance—intensifies the strange influence of the silence. You feel the force of the line I have quoted from Wordsworth—

The sleep that is among the lonely hills.

None of the travellers whom you can see crawling at your feet has the least conception of what is meant by the silent solitudes of the High Alps. To you, it is like a return to the stir of active life, when, after hours of lonely wandering, you return to hear the tinkling of the cow-bells below; to them the same sound is the ultimate limit of the habitable world.

Whilst your mind is properly toned by these influences, you become conscious of another fact, to which the common variety of tourists is necessarily insensible. You begin to find out for the first time what the mountains really are. On one side, you look back upon the huge reservoirs from which the Oberland glaciers descend. You see the vast stores from which the great rivers of Europe are replenished, the monstrous crawling masses that are carving the mountains into shape, and the gigantic bulwarks that separate two great quarters of the world. From below these wild regions are half invisible; they are masked by the outer line of mountains; and it is not till you are able to command them from some lofty point that you can appreciate the grandeur of the huge barriers, and the snow that is piled within their folds. There is another half of the view equally striking. Looking towards the north, the whole of Switzerland is couched at your feet; the Jura and the Black Forest lie on the far horizon. And then you know what is the nature of a really mountainous country. From below everything is seen in a kind of distorted perspective. The people of the valley naturally think that the valley is everything—that the country resembles old-fashioned maps, where a few sporadic lumps are distributed amongst towns and plains. The true proportions reveal themselves as you ascend. The valleys, you can now see, are nothing but narrow trenches scooped out amidst a tossing waste of mountain, just to carry off the drainage. The great ridges run hither and thither, having it all their own way, wild and untamable regions of rock or open grass or forest, at whose feet the valleys exist on sufferance. Creeping about amongst the roots of the hills, you half miss the hills themselves; you quite fail to understand the massiveness of the mountain chains, and, therefore, the wonderful energy of the forces that have heaved the surface of the world into these distorted shapes. And it is to a half-conscious sense of the powers that must have been at work that a great part of the influence of mountain scenery is due. Geologists tell us that a theory of catastrophes is unphilosophical; but, whatever may be the scientific truth, our minds are impressed as though we were witnessing the results of some incredible convulsion. At Stonehenge we ask what human beings could have erected these strange grey monuments, and in the mountains we instinctively ask what force can have carved out the Matterhorn, and placed the Wetterhorn on its gigantic pedestal. Now, it is not till we reach some commanding point that we realise the amazing extent of country over which the solid ground has been shaking and heaving itself in irresistible tumult.

Something, it is true, of this last effect may be seen from such mountains as the Rigi or the Faulhorn. There, too, one seems to be at the centre of a vast sphere, the earth bending up in a cup-like form to meet the sky, and the blue vault above stretching in an arch majestical by its enormous extent. There you seem to see a sensible fraction of the world at your feet. But the effect is far less striking when other mountains obviously look down upon you; when, as it were, you are looking at the waves of the great ocean of hills merely from the crest of one of the waves themselves, and not from some lighthouse that rises far over their heads; for the Wetterhorn, like the Eiger, Mönch, and Jungfrau, owes one great beauty to the fact that it is on the edge of the lower country, and stands between the real giants and the crowd of inferior, though still enormous, masses in attendance upon them. And, in the next place, your mind is far better adapted to receive impressions of sublimity when you are alone, in a silent region, with a black sky above and giant cliffs all round; with a sense still in your mind, if not of actual danger, still of danger that would become real with the slightest relaxation of caution, and with the world divided from you by hours of snow and rock.

I will go no further, not because I have no more to say, but because descriptions of scenery soon become wearisome, and because I have, I hope, said enough to show that the mountaineer may boast of some intellectual pleasures; that he is not a mere scrambler, but that he looks for poetical impressions, as well as for such small glory as his achievements may gain in a very small circle. Something of what he gains fortunately sticks by him: he does not quite forget the mountain language; his eye still recognises the space and the height and the glory of the lofty mountains. And yet there is some pain in wandering ghostlike among the scenes of his earlier pleasures. For my part, I try in vain to hug myself in a sense of comfort. I turn over in bed when I hear the stamping of heavily nailed shoes along the passage of an inn about 2 A.M. I feel the skin of my nose complacently when I see others returning with a glistening tight aspect about that unluckily prominent feature, and know that in a day or two it will be raw and blistered and burning. I think, in a comfortable inn at night, of the miseries of those who are trying to sleep in damp hay, or on hard boards of châlets, at once cold and stuffy and haunted by innumerable fleas. I congratulate myself on having a whole skin and unfractured bones, and on the small danger of ever breaking them over an Alpine precipice. But yet I secretly know that these consolations are feeble. It is little use to avoid early rising and discomfort, and even fleas, if one also loses the pleasures to which they were the sauce—rather too *piquante* a sauce occasionally, it must be admitted. The philosophy is all very well which recommends moderate enjoyment, regular exercise, and a careful avoidance of risk and over-excitement. That is, it is all very well so long as risk and excitement and immoderate enjoyment are out of your power; but it does not stand the test of looking on and seeing them just beyond your reach. In time, no doubt, a man may grow calm; he may learn to enjoy the pleasures and the exquisite beauties of the lower regions—though they, too, are most fully enjoyed when they have a contrast with beauties of a different, and pleasures of a keener excitement. When first debarred, at any rate, one feels like a balloon full of gas, and fixed by immovable ropes to the prosaic ground. It is pleasant to lie on one's back in a bed of rhododendrons, and look up to a mountain top peering at one from above a bank of cloud; but it is pleasantest when one has qualified oneself for repose by climbing the peak the day before and becoming familiar with its terrors and its beauties. In time, doubtless, one may get reconciled to anything; one may settle down to be a caterpillar, even after one has known the pleasures of being a butterfly; one may become philosophical, and have one's clothes let out; and even in time, perhaps—though it is almost too terrible to contemplate—be content with a mule or a carriage, or that lowest depth to which human beings can sink, and for which the English language happily affords no name, a *chaise à porteurs:* and even in such degradation the memory of better times may be pleasant; for I doubt much whether it is truth the poet sings—

That a sorrow's crown of sorrow is remembering happier things.

Certainly, to a philosophical mind, the sentiment is doubtful. For my part, the fate which has cut me off, if I may use the expression, in the flower of my youth, and doomed me to be a non-climbing animal in future, is one which ought to exclude grumbling. I cannot indicate it more plainly, for I might so make even the grumbling in which I have already indulged look like a sin. I can only say that there are some very delightful things in which it is possible to discover an infinitesimal drop of bitterness, and that the mountaineer who undertakes to cut himself off from his favourite pastime, even for reasons which he will admit in his wildest moods to be more than amply sufficient, must expect at times to feel certain pangs of regret, however quickly they may be smothered.

FOOTNOTES:

[Footnote 33: From "The Playground of Europe," 1871.]

BEHAVIOR[34]

RALPH WALDO EMERSON

The soul which animates nature is not less significantly published in the figure, movement, and gesture of animated bodies, than in its last vehicle of articulate speech. This silent and subtle language is Manners; not *what*, but *how*. Life expresses. A statue has no tongue, and needs none. Good tableaux do not need declamation. Nature tells every secret once. Yes, but in man she tells it all the time, by form, attitude, gesture, mien, face, and parts of the face, and by the whole action of the machine. The visible carriage or action of the individual, as resulting from his organization and his will combined, we call manners. What are they but thought entering the hands and feet, controlling the movements of the body, the speech and behavior?

There is always a best way of doing everything, if it be to boil an egg. Manners are the happy ways of doing things; each once a stroke of genius or of love,—now repeated and hardened into usage. They form at last a rich varnish, with which the routine of life is washed, and its details adorned. If they are superficial, so are the dew-drops which give such a depth to the morning meadows. Manners are very communicable: men catch them from each other. Consuelo, in the romance, boasts of the lessons she had given the nobles in manners, on the stage: and, in real life, Talma taught Napoleon the arts of behavior. Genius invents fine manners, which the baron and the baroness copy very fast, and, by the advantage of a palace, better the instruction. They stereotype the lesson they have learned into a mode.

The power of manners is incessant,—an element as unconcealable as fire. The nobility cannot in any country be disguised, and no more in a republic or a democracy than in a kingdom. No man can resist their influence. There are certain manners which are learned in good society, of that force, that, if a person have them, he or she must be considered, and is everywhere welcome, though without beauty, or wealth, or genius. Give a boy address and accomplishments, and you give him the mastery of palaces and fortunes where he goes. He has not the trouble of earning or owning them; they solicit him to enter and possess. We send girls of a timid, retreating disposition to the boarding-school, to the riding-school, to the ballroom, or wheresoever they can come into acquaintance and nearness of leading persons of their own sex; where they might learn address, and see it near at hand. The power of a woman of fashion to lead, and also to daunt and repel, derives from their belief that she knows resources and behaviors not known to them; but when these have mastered her secret, they learn to confront her, and recover their self-possession.

Every day bears witness to their gentle rule. People who would obtrude, now do not obtrude. The mediocre circle learns to demand that which belongs to a high state of nature or of culture. Your manners are always under examination, and by committees little suspected,—a police in citizen's clothes,—but are awarding or denying you very high prizes when you least think of it.

We talk much of utilities,—but 'tis our manners that associate us. In hours of business, we go to him who knows, or has, or does this or that which we want, and we do not let our taste or feeling stand in the way. But this activity over, we return to the indolent state, and wish for those we can be at ease with; those who will go where we go, whose manners do not offend us, whose social tone chimes with ours. When we reflect on their persuasive and cheering force; how they recommend, prepare, and draw people together; how, in all clubs, manners make the members; how manners make the fortune of the ambitious youth; that, for the most part, his manners marry him, and, for the most part, he marries manners; when we think what keys they are, and to what secrets; what high lessons and inspiring tokens of character they convey; and what divination is required in us, for the reading of this fine telegraph; we see what range the subject has, and what relations to convenience, power, and beauty.

Their first service is very low,—when they are the minor morals; but 'tis the beginning of civility,—to make us, I mean, endurable to each other. We prize them for their rough-plastic, abstergent force; to get people out of the quadruped state; to get them washed, clothed, and set up on end; to slough their animal husks and habits; compel them to be clean; overawe their spite and meanness, teach them to stifle the base, and choose the generous expression, and make them know how much happier the generous behaviors are.

Bad behavior the laws cannot reach. Society is invested with rude, cynical, restless, and frivolous persons who prey upon the rest, and whom a public opinion concentrated into good manners, forms accepted by the sense of all, can reach;—the contradictors and railers at public and private tables, who are like terriers, who conceive it the duty of a dog of honor to growl at any passer-by, and do the honors of the house by barking him out of sight;—I have seen men who neigh like a horse when you contradict them, or say something which they do not understand;—then the overbold, who make their own invitation to your hearth; the persevering talker, who gives you his society in large, saturating doses; the pitiers of themselves,—a perilous class; the frivolous Asmodeus, who relies on you to find him in ropes of sand to twist; the monotones; in short, every stripe of absurdity;—these are social inflictions which the magistrate cannot cure or defend you from, and which must be intrusted to the restraining force of custom, and proverbs, and familiar rules of behavior impressed on young people in their school-days.

In the hotels on the banks of the Mississippi, they print, or used to print, among the rules of the house, that "No gentleman can be permitted to come to the public table without his coat;" and in the same country, in the pews of the churches, little placards plead with the worshipper against the fury of expectoration. Charles Dickens self-sacrificingly undertook the reformation of our American manners in unspeakable particulars. I think the lesson was not quite lost; that it held bad manners up, so that the churls could see the deformity. Unhappily, the book had its own deformities. It ought not to need to print in a reading room a caution to strangers not to speak loud; nor to persons who look over fine engravings, that they should be handled like cobwebs and butterflies' wings; nor to persons who look at marble statues, that they shall not smite them with canes. But, even in the perfect civilization of this city, such cautions are not quite needless in the Athenaeum and City Library.

Manners are factitious, and grow out of circumstances as well as out of character. If you look at the pictures of patricians and of peasants, of different periods and countries, you will see how well they match the same classes in our towns. The modern aristocrat not only is well drawn in Titian's Venetian doges, and in Roman coins and statues, but also in the pictures which Commodore Perry brought home of dignitaries in Japan. Broad lands and great interests not only arrive to such heads as can manage them, but form manners of power. A keen eye, too, will see nice gradations of rank, or see in the manners the degree of homage the party is wont to receive. A prince who is accustomed every day to be courted and deferred to by the highest grandees, acquires a corresponding expectation, and a becoming mode of receiving and replying to this homage.

There are always exceptional people and modes. English grandees affect to be farmers. Claverhouse is a fop, and, under the finish of dress, and levity of behavior, hides the terror of his war. But Nature and Destiny are honest, and never fail to leave their mark, to hang out a sign for each and for every quality. It is much to conquer one's face, and perhaps the ambitious youth thinks he has got the whole secret when he has learned that disengaged manners are commanding. Don't be deceived by a facile exterior. Tender men sometimes have strong wills. We had, in Massachusetts, an old statesman, who had sat all his life in courts and in chairs of state, without overcoming an extreme irritability of face, voice, and bearing: when he spoke, his voice would not serve him; it cracked, it broke, it wheezed, it piped;—little cared he; he knew that it had got to pipe, or wheeze, or screech his argument and his indignation. When he sat down, after speaking, he seemed in a sort of fit, and held on to his chair with both hands: but underneath all this irritability was a puissant will, firm and advancing, and a memory in which lay in order and method, like geologic strata, every fact of his history, and under the control of his will.

Manners are partly factitious, but, mainly, there must be capacity for culture in the blood. Else all culture is vain. The obstinate prejudice in favor of blood, which lies at the base of the feudal and monarchical fabrics of the old world, has some reason in common experience. Every man,—mathematician, artist, soldier, or merchant,—looks with confidence for some traits and talents in his own child, which he would not dare to presume in the child of a stranger. The Orientalists are very orthodox on this point. "Take a thorn-bush," said the emir Abdel-Kader, "and sprinkle it for a whole year with water, it will yield nothing but thorns. Take a date-tree, leave it without culture, and it will always produce dates. Nobility is the date-tree, and the Arab populace is a bush of thorns."

A main fact in the history of manners is the wonderful expressiveness of the human body. If it were made of glass, or of air, and the thoughts were written on steel tablets within, it could not publish more truly its meaning than now. Wise men read very sharply all your private history in your look and gait and behavior. The whole economy of nature is bent on expression. The tell-tale body is all tongues. Men are like Geneva watches with crystal faces which expose the whole movement. They carry the liquor of life flowing up and down in these beautiful bottles, and announcing to the curious how it is with them. The face and eyes reveal what the spirit is doing, how old it is, what aims it has. The eyes indicate the antiquity of the soul, or through how many forms it has already ascended. It almost violates the proprieties, if we say above the breath here what the confessing eyes do not hesitate to utter to every street passenger.

Man cannot fix his eye on the sun, and so far seems imperfect. In Siberia, a late traveller found men who could see the satellites of Jupiter with their unarmed eye. In some respects the animals excel us. The birds have a longer sight, beside the advantage by their wings of a higher observatory. A cow can bid her calf, by secret signal, probably of the eye, to run away, or to lie down and hide itself. The jockeys say of certain horses, that "they look over the whole ground." The outdoor life, and hunting, and labor, give equal vigor to the human eye. A farmer looks out at you as strong as the horse; his eye-beam is like the stroke of a staff. An eye can threaten like a loaded and levelled gun, or can insult like hissing or kicking; or, in its altered mood, by beams of kindness, it can make the heart dance with joy.

The eye obeys exactly the action of the mind. When a thought strikes us, the eyes fix, and remain gazing at a distance; in enumerating the names of persons or of countries, as France, Germany, Spain, Turkey, the eyes wink at each new name. There is no nicety of learning sought by the mind, which the eyes do not vie in acquiring. "An artist," said Michael Angelo, "must have his measuring tools not in the hand, but in the eye;" and there is no end to the catalogue of its performances, whether in indolent vision (that of health and beauty) or in strained vision (that of art and labor).

Eyes are bold as lions,—roving, running, leaping, here and there, far and near. They speak all languages. They wait for no introduction; they are no Englishmen; ask no leave of age or rank; they respect neither poverty nor riches, neither learning nor power, nor virtue, nor sex, but intrude, and come again, and go through and through you, in a moment of time. What inundation of life and thought is discharged from one soul into another through them! The glance is natural magic. The mysterious communication established across a house between two entire strangers moves all the springs of wonder. The communication by the glance is in the greatest part not subject to the control of the will. It is the bodily symbol of identity of nature. We look into the eyes to know if this other form is another self, and the eyes will not lie, but make a faithful confession what inhabitant is there. The revelations are sometimes terrific. The confession of a low, usurping devil is there made, and the observer shall seem to feel the stirring of owls, and bats, and horned hoofs, where he looked for innocence and simplicity. 'Tis remarkable, too, that the spirit that appears at the windows of the house does at once invest himself in a new form of his own to the mind of the beholder.

The eyes of men converse as much as their tongues, with the advantage, that the ocular dialect needs no dictionary, but is understood all the world over. When the eyes say one thing, and the tongue another, a practised man relies on the language of the first. If the man is off his center, the eyes show it. You can read in the eyes of your companion, whether your argument hits him, though his tongue will not confess it. There is a look by which a man shows he is going to say a good thing, and a look when he has said it. Vain and forgotten are all the fine offers and offices of hospitality, if there is no holiday in the eye. How many furtive inclinations avowed by the eye, though dissembled by the lips! One comes away from a company, in which, it may easily happen, he has said nothing, and no important remark has been addressed to him, and yet, if in sympathy with the society he shall not have a sense of this fact, such a stream of life has been flowing into him, and out from him, through the eyes. There are eyes, to be sure, that give no more admission into the man than blue-berries. Others are liquid and deep, —wells that a man might fall into;—others are aggressive and devouring, seem to call out the police, take all too much notice, and require crowded Broadways, and the security of millions, to protect individuals against them. The military eye I meet, now darkly sparkling under clerical, now under rustic brows. 'Tis the city of Lacedaemon; 'tis a stack of bayonets. There are asking eyes, asserting eyes, prowling eyes; and eyes full of fate,—some of good, and some of sinister omen. The alleged power to charm down insanity, or ferocity in beasts, is a power behind the eye. It must be a victory achieved in the will before it can be signified in the eye. 'Tis very certain that each man carries in his eye the exact indication of his rank in the immense scale of men, and we are always learning to read it. A complete man should need no auxiliaries to his personal presence. Whoever looked on him would consent to his will, being certified that his aims were generous and universal. The reason why men do not obey us, is because they see the mud at the bottom of our eye.

If the organ of sight is such a vehicle of power, the other features have their own. A man finds room in the few square inches of the face for the traits of all his ancestors; for the expression of all his history, and his wants. The sculptor, and Winckelmann, and Lavater, will tell you how significant a feature is the nose; how its forms express strength or weakness of will, and good or bad temper. The nose of Julius Caesar, of Dante, and of Pitt, suggest "the terrors of the beak." What refinement, and what limitations, the teeth betray! "Beware you don't laugh," said the wise mother, "for then you show all your faults."

Balzac left in manuscript a chapter, which he called "*Théorie de la démarche*,"[35] in which he says: "The look, the voice, the respiration, and the attitude or walk, are identical. But, as it has not been given to man, the power to stand guard, at once, over these four different simultaneous expressions of his thought, watch that one which speaks out the truth, and you will know the whole man."

Palaces interest us mainly in the exhibition of manners, which, in the idle and expensive society dwelling in them, are raised to a high art. The maxim of courts is, that manner is power. A calm and resolute bearing, a polished speech, an embellishment of trifles, and the art of hiding all uncomfortable feeling, are essential to the courtier: and Saint Simon, and Cardinal de Retz, and Roederer, and an encyclopaedia of *Mémoires,* will instruct you, if you wish, in those potent secrets. Thus, it is a point of pride with kings to remember faces and names. It is reported of one prince, that his head had the air of leaning downwards, in order not to humble the crowd. There are people who come in ever like a child with a piece of good news. It was said of the late Lord Holland, that he always came down to breakfast with the air of a man who had just met with some signal good-fortune. In *Notre Dame*, the grandee took his place on the dais, with the look of one who is thinking of something else. But we must not peep and eavesdrop at palace-doors.

Fine manners need the support of fine manners in others. A scholar may be a well-bred man, or he may not. The enthusiast is introduced to polished scholars in society, and is chilled and silenced by finding himself not in their element. They all have somewhat which he has not, and, it seems, ought to have. But if he finds the scholar apart from his companions, it is then the enthusiast's turn, and the scholar has no defence, but must deal on his terms. Now they must fight the battle out on their private strengths. What is the talent of that character so common,—the successful man of the world,—in all marts, senates, and drawing-rooms? Manners: mariners of power; sense to see his advantage, and manners up to it. See him approach his man. He knows that troops behave as they are handled at first;—that is his cheap secret; just what happens to every two persons who meet on any affair,—one instantly perceives that he has the key of the situation, that his will comprehends the other's will, as the cat does the mouse; and he has only to use courtesy, and furnish good-natured reasons to his victim to cover up the chain, lest he be shamed into resistance.

The theater in which this science of manners has a formal importance is not with us a court, but dress-circles, wherein, after the close of the day's business, men and women meet at leisure, for mutual entertainment, in ornamented drawing-rooms. Of course, it has every variety of attraction and merit; but, to earnest persons, to youths or maidens who have great objects at heart, we cannot extol it highly. A well-dressed, talkative company, where each is bent to amuse the other,—yet the high-born Turk who came hither fancied that every woman seemed to be suffering for a chair; that all the talkers were brained and exhausted by the deoxygenated air; it spoiled the best persons: it put all on stilts. Yet here are the secret biographies written and read. The aspect of that man is repulsive; I do not wish to deal with him. The other is irritable, shy, and on his guard. The youth looks humble and manly: I choose him. Look on this woman. There is not beauty, nor brilliant sayings, nor distinguished power, to serve you; but all see her gladly; her whole air and impression are healthful. Here come the sentimentalists, and the invalids. Here is Elise, who caught cold in coming into the world, and has always increased it since. Here are creep-mouse manners, and thievish manners. "Look at Northcote," said Fuseli; "he looks like a rat that has seen a cat." In the shallow company, easily excited, easily tired, here is the columnar Bernard: the Alleghanies do not express more repose than his behavior. Here are the sweet following eyes of Cecile: it seemed always that she demanded the heart. Nothing can be more excellent in kind than the Corinthian grace of Gertrude's manners, and yet Blanche, who has no manners, has better manners than she; for the movements of Blanche are the sallies of a spirit which is sufficient for the moment, and she can afford to express every thought by instant action.

Manners have been somewhat cynically defined to be a contrivance of wise men to keep fools at a distance. Fashion is shrewd to detect those who do not belong to her train, and seldom wastes her attentions. Society is very swift in its instincts, and, if you do not belong to it, resists and sneers at you; or quietly drops you. The first weapon enrages the party attacked; the second is still more effective, but is not to be resisted, as the date of the transaction is not easily found. People grow up and grow old under this infliction, and never suspect the truth, ascribing the solitude which acts on them very injuriously to any cause but the right one.

The basis of good manners is self-reliance. Necessity is the law of all who are not self-possessed. Those who are not self-possessed, obtrude, and pain us. Some men appear to feel that they belong to a Pariah caste. They fear to offend, they bend and apologize, and walk through life with a timid step. As we sometimes dream that we are in a well-dressed company without any coat, so Godfrey acts ever as if he suffered from some mortifying circumstance. The hero should find himself at home, wherever he is; should impart comfort by his own security and good-nature to all beholders. The hero is suffered to be himself. A person of strong mind comes to perceive that for him an immunity is secured so long as he renders to society that service which is native and proper to him,—an immunity from all the observances, yea, and duties, which society so tyrannically imposes on the rank and file of its members. "Euripides," says Aspasia, "has not the fine manners of Sophocles; but,"—she adds good-humoredly, "the movers and masters of our souls have surely a right to throw out their limbs as carelessly as they please on the world that belongs to them, and before the creatures they have animated."[36]

Manners require time, as nothing is more vulgar than haste. Friendship should be surrounded with ceremonies and respects, and not crushed into corners. Friendship requires more time than poor busy men can usually command. Here comes to me Roland, with a delicacy of sentiment leading and inwrapping him like a divine cloud or holy ghost. Tis a great destitution to both that this should not be entertained with large leisures, but, contrariwise, should be balked by importunate affairs.

But through this lustrous varnish the reality is ever shining. 'Tis hard to keep the *what* from breaking through this pretty painting of the *how*. The core will come to the surface. Strong will and keen perception overpower old manners and create new; and the thought of the present moment has a greater value than all the past. In persons of character, we do not remark manners, because of their instantaneousness. We are surprised by the thing done, out of all power to watch the way of it. Yet nothing is more charming than to recognize the great style which runs through the actions of such. People masquerade before us in their fortunes, titles, offices, and connections, as academic or civil presidents, or senators, or professors, or great lawyers, and impose on the frivolous, and a good deal on each other, by these fames. At least, it is a point of prudent good manners to treat these reputations tenderly, as if they were merited. But the sad realist knows these fellows at a glance, and they know him; as when in Paris the chief of the police enters a ballroom, so many diamonded pretenders shrink and make themselves as inconspicuous as they can, or give him a supplicating look as they pass. "I had received," said a sybil, "I had received at birth the fatal gift of penetration:"—and these Cassandras are always born.

Manners impress as they indicate real power. A man who is sure of his point, carries a broad and contented expression, which everybody reads. And you cannot rightly train one to an air and manner, except by making him the kind of man of whom that manner is the natural expression. Nature for ever puts a premium on reality. What is done for effect, is seen to be done for effect; what is done for love, is felt to be done for love. A man inspires affection and honor, because he was not lying in wait for these. The things of a man for which we visit him, were done in the dark and the cold. A little integrity is better than any career. So deep are the sources of this surface-action, that even the size of your companion seems to vary with his freedom of thought. Not only is he larger, when at ease, and his thoughts generous, but everything around him becomes variable with expression. No carpenter's rule, no rod and chain, will measure the dimensions of any house or house-lot: go into the house: if the proprietor is constrained and deferring, 'tis of no importance how large his house, how beautiful his grounds,—you quickly come to the end of all; but if the man is self-possessed, happy, and at home, his house is deep-founded, indefinitely large and interesting, the roof and dome buoyant as the sky. Under the humblest roof, the commonest person in plain clothes sits there massive, cheerful, yet formidable, like the Egyptian colossi.

Neither Aristotle, nor Leibnitz, nor Junius, nor Champollion has set down the grammar-rules of this dialect, older than Sanscrit; but they who cannot yet read English, can read this. Men take each other's measure when they meet for the first time,—and every time they meet. How do they get this rapid knowledge, even before they speak, of each other's power and dispositions? One would say, that the persuasion of their speech is not in what they say,—or, that men do not convince by their argument,—but by their personality, by who they are, and what they said and did heretofore. A man already strong is listened to, and everything he says is applauded. Another opposes him with sound argument, but the argument is scouted, until by-and-by it gets into the mind of some weighty person; then it begins to tell on the community.

Self-reliance is the basis of behavior, as it is the guaranty that the powers are not squandered in too much demonstration. In this country, where school education is universal, we have a superficial culture, and a profusion of reading and writing and expression. We parade our nobilities in poems and orations, instead of working them up into happiness. There is a whisper out of the ages to him who can understand it,—"Whatever is known to thyself alone, has always very great value." There is some reason to believe, that, when a man does not write his poetry, it escapes by other vents through him, instead of the one vent of writing; clings to his form and manners, whilst poets have often nothing poetical about them except their verses. Jacobi said that, "when a man has fully expressed his thought, he has somewhat less possession of it." One would say, the rule is,—What a man is irresistibly urged to say, helps him and us. In explaining his thought to others, he explains it to himself: but when he opens it for show, it corrupts him.

Society is the stage on which manners are shown; novels are their literature. Novels are the journal or record of manners; and the new importance of these books derives from the fact, that the novelist begins to penetrate the surface, and treats this part of life more worthily. The novels used to be all alike, and had a quite vulgar tone. The novels used to lead us on to a foolish interest in the fortunes of the boy and girl they described. The boy was to be raised from a humble to a high position. He was in want of a wife and a castle, and the object of the story was to supply him with one or both. We watched sympathetically, step by step, his climbing, until, at last, the point is gained, the wedding day is fixed, and we follow the gala procession home to the castle, when the doors are slammed in our face, and the poor reader is left outside in the cold, not enriched by so much as an idea, or a virtuous impulse.

But the victories of character are instant, and victories for all. Its greatness enlarges all. We are fortified by every heroic anecdote. The novels are as useful as Bibles, if they teach you the secret, that the best of life is conversation, and the greatest success is confidence, or perfect understanding between sincere people. 'Tis a French definition of friendship, *rien que s'entendre,* good understanding. The highest compact we can make with our fellow is,—"Let there be truth between us two for evermore." That is the charm in all good novels, as it is the charm in all good histories, that the heroes mutually understand, from the first, and deal loyally, and with a profound trust in each other. It is sublime to feel and say of another, I need never meet, or speak, or write to him: we need not reinforce ourselves, or send tokens of remembrance: I rely on him as on myself: if he did thus or thus, I know it was right.

In all the superior people I have met, I notice directness, truth spoken more truly, as if everything of obstruction, of malformation, had been trained away. What have they to conceal? What have they to exhibit? Between simple and noble persons, there is always a quick intelligence: they recognize at sight, and meet on a better ground than the talents and skills they may chance to possess, namely, on sincerity and uprightness. For, it is not what talents or genius a man has, but how he is to his talents, that constitutes friendship and character. The man that stands by himself, the universe stands by him also. It is related of the monk Basle, that, being excommunicated by the Pope, he was, at his death, sent in charge of an angel to find a fit place of suffering in hell; but, such was the eloquence and good-humor of the monk, that, wherever he went, he was received gladly, and civilly treated, even by the most uncivil angels: and, when he came to discourse with them, instead of contradicting or forcing him, they took his part, and adopted his manners: and even good angels came from far to see him, and take up their abode with him. The angel that was sent to find a place of torment for him, attempted to remove him to a worse pit, but with no better success; for such was the contented spirit of the monk, that he found something to praise in every place and company, though in hell, and made a kind of heaven of it. At last the escorting angel returned with his prisoner to them that sent him, saying, that no phlegethon could be found that would burn him; for that, in whatever condition, Basle remained incorrigibly Basle. The legend says, his sentence was remitted, and he was allowed to go into heaven, and was canonized as a saint.

There is a stroke of magnanimity in the correspondence of Bonaparte with his brother Joseph, when the latter was King of Spain, and complained that he missed in Napoleon's letters the affectionate tone which had marked their childish correspondence. "I am sorry," replies Napoleon, "you think you shall find your brother again only in the Elysian Fields. It is natural that at forty he should not feel towards you as he did at twelve. But his feelings towards you have greater truth and strength. His friendship has the features of his mind."

How much we forgive to those who yield us the rare spectacle of heroic manners! We will pardon them the want of books, of arts, and even of the gentler virtues. How tenaciously we remember them! Here is a lesson which I brought along with me in boyhood from the Latin School, and which ranks with the best of Roman anecdotes. Marcus Scaurus was accused by Quintus Varius Hispanus, that he had excited the allies to take arms against the Republic. But he, full of firmness and gravity, defended himself in this manner: "Quintus Varius Hispanus alleges that Marcus Scaurus, President of the Senate, excited the allies to arms: Marcus Scaurus,

President of the Senate, denies it. There is no witness. Which do you believe, Romans?" "*Utri creditis, Quirites?*" When he had said these words, he was absolved by the assembly of the people.

I have seen manners that make a similar impression with personal beauty; that give the like exhilaration, and refine us like that; and, in memorable experiences, they are suddenly better than beauty, and make that superfluous and ugly. But they must be marked by fine perception, the acquaintance with real beauty. They must always show self-control: you shall not be facile, apologetic, or leaky, but king over your word; and every gesture and action shall indicate power at rest. Then they must be inspired by the good heart. There is no beautifier of complexion, or form, or behavior, like the wish to scatter joy and not pain around us. 'Tis good to give a stranger a meal, or a night's lodging. 'Tis better to be hospitable to his good meaning and thought, and give courage to a companion. We must be as courteous to a man as we are to a picture, which we are willing to give the advantage of a good light. Special precepts are not to be thought of: the talent of well-doing contains them all. Every hour will show a duty as paramount as that of my whim just now; and yet I will write it,—that there is one topic peremptorily forbidden to all well-bred, to all rational mortals, namely, their distempers. If you have not slept, or if you have slept, or if you have headache, or sciatica, or leprosy, or thunder-stroke, I beseech you, by all angels, to hold your peace, and not pollute the morning, to which all the housemates bring serene and pleasant thoughts, by corruption and groans. Come out in the azure. Love the day. Do not leave the sky out of your landscape. The oldest and the most deserving person should come very modestly into any newly awaked company, respecting the divine communications, out of which all must be presumed to have newly come. An old man who added an elevating culture to a large experience of life, said to me, "When you come into the room, I think I will study how to make humanity beautiful to you."

As respects the delicate question of culture, I do not think that any other than negative rules can be laid down. For positive rules, for suggestion, nature alone inspires it. Who dare assume to guide a youth, a maid, to perfect manners?—the golden mean is so delicate, difficult,—say frankly unattainable. What finest hands would not be clumsy to sketch the genial precepts of the young girl's demeanor? The chances seem infinite against success; and yet success is continually attained. There must not be secondariness, and 'tis a thousand to one that her air and manner will at once betray that she is not primary, but that there is some other one or many of her class, to whom she habitually postpones herself. But nature lifts her easily, and without knowing it, over these impossibilities, and we are continually surprised with graces and felicities not only unteachable, but undescribable.

FOOTNOTES:

[Footnote 34: Chapter V of "The Conduct of Life," 1860.]

[Footnote 35: Theory of gait and demeanor.]

[Footnote 36: From Landor's "Pericles and Aspasia."]

MANNERS AND FASHION[37]

HERBERT SPENCER

Some who shun drawing-rooms do so from inability to bear the restraints prescribed by a genuine refinement, and they would be greatly improved by being kept under these restraints. But it is not less true that, by adding to the legitimate restraints, which are based on convenience and a regard for others, a host of factitious restraints based only on convention, the refining discipline, which would else have been borne with benefit, is rendered unbearable, and so misses its end. Excess of government invariably defeats itself by driving away those to be governed. And if over all who desert its entertainments in disgust either at their emptiness or their formality, society thus loses its salutary influence—if such not only fail to receive that moral culture which the company of ladies, when rationally regulated, would give them, but, in default of other relaxation, are driven into habits and companionships which often end in gambling and drunkenness; must we not say that here, too, is an evil not to be passed over as insignificant?

Then consider what a blighting effect these multitudinous preparations and ceremonies have upon the pleasures they profess to subserve. Who, on calling to mind the occasions of his highest social enjoyments, does not find them to have been wholly informal, perhaps impromptu? How delightful a picnic of friends, who forget all observances save those dictated by good nature! How pleasant the little unpretended gatherings of book-societies, and the like; or those purely accidental meetings of a few people well known to each other! Then, indeed, we may see that "a man sharpeneth the countenance of his friend." Cheeks flush, and eyes sparkle. The witty grow brilliant, and even the dull are excited into saying good things. There is an overflow of topics; and the right thought, and the right words to put it in, spring up unsought. Grave alternates with gay: now serious converse, and now jokes, anecdotes, and playful raillery. Everyone's best nature is shown, everyone's best feelings are in pleasurable activity; and, for the time, life seems well worth having.

Go now and dress for some half-past eight dinner, or some ten o'clock "at home;" and present yourself in spotless attire, with every hair arranged to perfection. How great the difference! The enjoyment seems in the inverse ratio of the preparation. These figures, got up with such finish and precision, appear but half alive. They have frozen each other by their primness; and your faculties feel the numbing effects of the atmosphere the moment you enter it. All those thoughts, so nimble and so apt awhile since, have disappeared—have suddenly acquired a preternatural power of eluding you. If you venture a remark to your neighbour, there comes a trite rejoinder, and there it ends. No subject you can hit upon outlives half a dozen sentences. Nothing that is said excites any real interest in you; and you feel that all you say is listened to with apathy. By some strange magic, things that usually give pleasure seem to have lost all charm.

You have a taste for art. Weary of frivolous talk, you turn to the table, and find that the book of engravings and the portfolio of photographs are as flat as the conversation. You are fond of music. Yet the singing, good as it is, you hear with utter indifference; and say "Thank you" with a sense of being a profound hypocrite. Wholly at ease though you could be, for your own part, you find that your sympathies will not let you. You see young gentlemen feeling whether their ties are properly adjusted, looking vacantly round, and considering what they shall do next. You see ladies sitting disconsolately, waiting for some one to speak to them, and wishing they had the wherewith to occupy their fingers. You see the hostess standing about the doorway, keeping a factitious smile on her face, and racking her brain to find the requisite nothings with which to greet her guests as they enter. You see numberless traits of weariness and embarrassment; and, if you have any fellow-feeling, these cannot fail to produce a feeling of discomfort. The disorder is catching; and do what you will you cannot resist the general infection. You struggle against it; you make spasmodic efforts to be lively; but none of your sallies or your good stories do more than raise a simper or a forced laugh: intellect and feeling are alike asphyxiated. And when, at length, yielding to your disgust, you rush away, how great is the relief when you get into the fresh air, and see the stars! How you "Thank God, that's over!" and half resolve to avoid all such boredom for the future!

What, now, is the secret of this perpetual miscarriage and disappointment? Does not the fault lie with all these needless adjuncts—these elaborate dressings, these set forms, these expensive preparations, these many devices and arrangements that imply trouble and raise expectation? Who that has lived thirty years in the world has not discovered that Pleasure is coy; and must not be too directly pursued, but must be caught unawares? An air from a street-piano, heard while at work, will often gratify more than the choicest music played at a concert by the most accomplished musicians. A single good picture seen in a dealer's window, may give keener enjoyment than a whole exhibition gone through with catalogue and pencil. By the time we have got ready our elaborate apparatus by which to secure happiness, the happiness is gone. It is too subtle to be contained in these receivers, garnished with compliments, and fenced round with etiquette. The more we multiply and complicate appliances, the more certain are we to drive it away.

The reason is patent enough. These higher emotions to which social intercourse ministers, are of extremely complex nature; they consequently depend for their production upon very numerous conditions; the more numerous the conditions, the greater the liability that one or other of them will be disturbed, and the emotions consequently prevented. It takes a considerable misfortune to destroy appetite; but cordial sympathy with those around may be extinguished by a look or a word. Hence it follows, that the more multiplied the *unnecessary* requirements with which social intercourse is surrounded, the less likely are its pleasures to be achieved. It is difficult enough to fulfil continuously all the *essentials* to a pleasurable communion with others: how much more difficult, then, must it be continuously to fulfil a host of *non-essentials* also! It is, indeed, impossible. The attempt inevitably ends in the sacrifice of the first to the last—the essentials to the non-essentials. What chance is there of getting any genuine response from the lady who is thinking of your stupidity in taking her in to dinner on the wrong arm? How are you likely to have agreeable converse with the gentleman who is fuming internally because he is not placed next to the hostess? Formalities, familiar as they may become, necessarily occupy attention—necessarily multiply the occasions for mistake, misunderstanding, and jealousy, on the part of one or other—necessarily distract all minds from the thoughts and feelings that should occupy them—necessarily, therefore, subvert those conditions under which only any sterling intercourse is to be had.

And this indeed is the fatal mischief which these conventions entail—a mischief to which every other is secondary. They destroy those highest of our pleasures which they profess to subserve. All institutions are alike in this, that however useful, and needful even, they originally were, they not only in the end cease to be so, but become detrimental. While humanity is growing, they continue fixed; daily get more mechanical and unvital; and by and by tend to strangle what they before preserved. It is not simply that they become corrupt and fail to act; they become obstructions. Old forms of government finally grow so oppressive, that they must be thrown off even at the risk of reigns of terror. Old creeds end in being dead formulas, which no longer aid but distort and arrest the general mind; while the State-churches administering them, come to be instruments for subsidising conservatism and repressing progress. Old schemes of education, incarnated in public schools and colleges, continue filling the heads of new generations with what has become relatively useless knowledge, and, by consequence, excluding knowledge which is useful. Not an organisation of any kind—political, religious, literary, philanthropic—but what, by its ever-multiplying regulations, its accumulating wealth, its yearly addition of officers, and the creeping into it of patronage and party feeling, eventually loses its original spirit, and sinks into a mere lifeless mechanism, worked with a view to private ends—a mechanism which not merely fails of its first purpose, but is a positive hindrance to it.

Thus is it, too, with social usages. We read of the Chinese that they have "ponderous ceremonies transmitted from time immemorial," which make social intercourse a burden. The court forms prescribed by monarchs for their own exaltation, have, in all times and places, ended in consuming the comfort of their lives. And so the artificial observances of the dining-room and saloon, in proportion as they are many and strict, extinguish that agreeable communion which they were originally intended to secure. The dislike with which people commonly speak of society that is "formal," and "stiff," and "ceremonious," implies the general recognition of this fact; and this recognition, logically developed, involves that all usages of behaviour which are not based on natural requirements, are injurious. That these conventions defeat their own ends is no new assertion. Swift, criticising the manners of his day, says—"Wise men are often more uneasy at the over-civility of these refiners than they could possibly be in the conversation of peasants and mechanics."

But it is not only in these details that the self-defeating action of our arrangements is traceable: it is traceable in the very substance and nature of them. Our social intercourse, as commonly managed, is a mere semblance of the reality sought. What is it that we want? Some sympathetic converse with our fellow-creatures: some converse that shall not be mere dead words, but the vehicle of living thoughts and feelings—converse in which the eyes and the face shall speak, and the tones of the voice be full of meaning—converse which shall make us feel no longer alone, but shall draw us closer to another, and double our own emotions by adding another's to them. Who is there that has not, from time to time, felt how cold and flat is all this talk about politics and science, and the new books and the new men, and how a genuine utterance of fellow-feeling outweighs the whole of it? Mark the words of Bacon:—"For a crowd is not a company, and faces are but a gallery of pictures, and talk but a tinkling cymbal, where there is no love."

If this be true, then it is only after acquaintance has grown into intimacy, and intimacy has ripened into friendship, that the real communion which men need becomes possible. A rationally-formed circle must consist almost wholly of those on terms of familiarity and regard, with but one or two strangers. What folly, then, underlies the whole system of our grand dinners, our "at homes," our evening parties—assemblages made up of many who never met before, many others who just bow to each other, many others who though familiar feel mutual indifference, with just a few real friends lost in the general mass! You need, but look round at the artificial expression of face, to see at once how it is. All have their disguises on; and how can there be sympathy between masks? No wonder that in private every one exclaims against the stupidity of these gatherings. No wonder that hostesses get them up rather because they must than because they wish. No wonder that the invited go less from the expectation of pleasure than from fear of giving offence. The whole thing is a gigantic mistake—an organised disappointment.

And then note, lastly, that in this case, as in all others, when an organisation has become effete and inoperative for its legitimate purpose, it is employed for quite other ones—quite opposite ones. What is the usual plea put in for giving and attending these tedious assemblies? "I admit that they are stupid and frivolous enough," replies every man to your criticisms; "but then, you know, one must keep up one's connections." And could you get from his wife a sincere answer, it would be—"Like you, I am sick of these frivolities; but then, we must get our daughters married." The one knows that there is a profession to push, a practice to gain, a business to extend: or parliamentary influence, or county patronage, or votes, or office, to be got: position, berths, favours, profit. The other's thoughts run upon husbands and settlements, wives and dowries. Worthless for their ostensible purpose of daily bringing human beings into pleasurable relations with each other, these cumbrous appliances of our social intercourse are now perseveringly kept in action with a view to the pecuniary and matrimonial results which they indirectly produce.

Who then shall say that the reform of our system of observances is unimportant? When we see how this system induces fashionable extravagance, with its entailed bankruptcy and ruin—when we mark how greatly it limits the amount of social intercourse among the less wealthy classes—when we find that many who most need to be disciplined by mixing with the refined are driven away by it, and led into dangerous and often fatal courses—when we count up the many minor evils it inflicts, the extra work which its costliness entails on all professional and mercantile men, the damage to public taste in dress and decoration by the setting up of its absurdities as standards for imitation, the injury to health indicated in the faces of its devotees at the close of the London season, the mortality of milliners and the like, which its sudden exigencies yearly involve;—and when to all these we add its fatal sin, that it blights, withers up, and kills that high enjoyment it professedly ministers to—that enjoyment which is a chief end of our hard struggling in life to obtain—shall we not conclude that to reform our system of etiquette and fashion, is an aim yielding to few in urgency?

There needs, then, a protestantism in social usages. Forms that have ceased to facilitate and have become obstructive—whether political, religious, or other—have ever to be swept away; and eventually are so swept away in all cases. Signs are not wanting that some change is at hand. A host of satirists, led on by Thackeray, have been for years engaged in bringing our sham-festivities, and our fashionable follies, into contempt; and in their candid moods, most men laugh at the frivolities with which they and the world in general are deluded. Ridicule has always been a revolutionary agent. That which is habitually assailed with sneers and sarcasms cannot long survive. Institutions that have lost their roots in men's respect and faith are doomed; and the day of their dissolution is not far off. The time is approaching, then, when our system of social observances must pass through some crisis, out of which it will come purified and comparatively simple.

How this crisis will be brought about, no one can with any certainty say. Whether by the continuance and increase of individual protests, or whether by the union of many persons for the practice and propagation of some better system, the future alone can decide. The influence of dissentients acting without cooperation, seems, under the present state of things, inadequate. Standing severally alone, and having no well-defined views; frowned on by conformists, and expostulated with even by those who secretly sympathise with them; subject to petty persecutions, and unable to trace any benefit produced by their example; they are apt, one by one, to give up their attempts as hopeless. The young convention-breaker eventually finds that he pays too heavily for his nonconformity. Hating, for example, everything that bears about it any remnant of servility, he determines, in the ardour of his independence, that he will uncover to no one. But what he means simply as a general protest, he finds that ladies interpret into a personal disrespect. Though he sees that, from the days of chivalry downwards, these marks of supreme consideration paid to the other sex have been but a hypocritical counterpart to the actual subjection in which men have held them—a pretended submission to compensate for a real domination; and though he sees that when the true dignity of women is recognised, the mock dignities given to them will be abolished, yet he does not like to be thus misunderstood, and so hesitates in his practice.

In other cases, again, his courage fails him. Such of his unconventionalities as can be attributed only to eccentricity, he has no qualms about: for, on the whole, he feels rather complimented than otherwise in being considered a disregarder of public opinion. But when they are liable to be put down to ignorance, to ill-breeding, or to poverty, he becomes a coward. However clearly the recent innovation of eating some kinds of fish with knife and fork proves the fork-and-bread practice to have had little but caprice for its basis, yet he dares not wholly ignore that practice while fashion partially maintains it. Though he thinks that a silk handkerchief is quite as appropriate for drawing-room use as a white cambric one, he is not altogether at ease in acting out his opinion. Then, too, be begins to perceive that his resistance to prescription brings round disadvantageous results which he had not calculated upon. He had expected that it would save him from a great deal of social intercourse of a frivolous kind—that it would offend the fools, but not the sensible people; and so would serve as a self-acting test by which those worth knowing would be separated from those not worth knowing. But the fools prove to be so greatly in the majority that, by offending them, he closes against himself nearly all the avenues through which the sensible people are to be reached. Thus he finds that his nonconformity is frequently misinterpreted; that there are but few directions in which he dares to carry it consistently out; that the annoyances and disadvantages which it brings upon him are greater than he anticipated; and that the chances of his doing any good are very remote. Hence he gradually loses resolution, and lapses, step by step, into the ordinary routine of observances.

Abortive as individual protests thus generally turn out, it may possibly be that nothing effectual will be done until there arises some organised resistance to this invisible despotism, by which our modes and habits are dictated. It may happen, that the government of Manners and Fashion will be rendered less tyrannical, as the political and religious governments have been, by some antagonistic union. Alike in Church and State, men's first emancipations from excess of restriction were achieved by numbers, bound together by a common creed, or a common political faith. What remained undone while there were but individual schismatics or rebels, was effected when there came to be many acting in concert. It is tolerably clear that these earliest instalments of freedom could not have been obtained in any other way; for so long as the feeling of personal independence was weak and the rule strong, there could never have been a sufficient number of separate dissentients to produce the desired results. Only in these later times, during which the secular and spiritual controls have been growing less coercive, and the tendency towards individual liberty greater, has it become possible for smaller and smaller sects and parties to fight against established creeds and laws; until now men may safely stand even alone in their antagonism.

The failure of individual nonconformity to customs, as above illustrated, suggests that an analogous series of changes may have to be gone through in this case also. It is true that the *lex non scripta* differs from the *lex scripta* in this, that, being unwritten, it is more readily altered; and that it has, from time to time, been quietly ameliorated. Nevertheless, we shall find that the analogy holds substantially good. For in this case, as in the others, the essential revolution is not the substituting of any one set of restraints for any other, but the limiting or abolishing the authority which prescribes restraints. Just as the fundamental change inaugurated by the Reformation, was not a superseding of one creed by another, but an ignoring of the arbiter who before dictated creeds—just as the fundamental change which Democracy long ago commenced, was not from this particular law to that, but from the despotism of one to the freedom of all; so, the parallel change yet to be wrought out in this supplementary government of which we are treating, is not the replacing of absurd usages by sensible ones, but the dethronement of that secret, irresponsible power which now imposes our usages, and the assertion of the right of all individuals to choose their own usages. In rules of living, a West-end clique is our Pope; and we are all papists, with but a mere sprinkling of heretics. On all who decisively rebel, comes down the penalty of excommunication, with its long catalogue of disagreeable and, indeed, serious consequences.

The liberty of the subject asserted in our constitution, and ever on the increase, has yet to be wrested from this subtler tyranny. The right of private judgment, which our ancestors wrung from the church, remains to be claimed from this dictator of our habits. Or, as before said, to free us from these idolatries and superstitious conformities, there has still to come a protestantism in social usages. Parallel, therefore, as is the change to be wrought out, it seems not improbable that it may be wrought out in an analogous way. That influence which solitary dissentients fail to gain, and that perseverance which they lack, may come into existence when they unite. That persecution which the world now visits upon them from mistaking their nonconformity for ignorance or disrespect, may diminish when it is seen to result from principle. The penalty which exclusion now entails may disappear when they become numerous enough to form visiting circles of their own. And when a successful stand has been made, and the brunt of the opposition has passed, that large amount of secret dislike to our observances which now pervades society, may manifest itself with sufficient power to effect the desired emancipation.

Whether such will be the process, time alone can decide. That community of origin, growth, supremacy, and decadence which we have found among all kinds of government, suggests a community in modes of change also. On the other hand, Nature often performs substantially similar operations, in ways apparently different. Hence these details can never be foretold.

Society, in all its developments, undergoes the process of exuviation. These old forms which it successively throws off, have all been once vitally united with it—have severally served as the protective envelopes within which a higher humanity was being evolved. They are cast aside only when they become hindrances—only when some inner and better envelope has been formed; and they bequeath to us all that there was in them of good. The periodical abolitions of tyrannical laws have left the administration of justice not only uninjured, but purified. Dead and buried creeds have not carried with them the essential morality they contained, which still exists, uncontaminated by the sloughs of superstition. And all that there is of justice and kindness and beauty, embodied in our cumbrous forms of etiquette, will live perennially when the forms themselves have been forgotten.

FOOTNOTES:

[Footnote 37: From "Illustrations of Universal Progress," 1864.]

TALK AND TALKERS[38]

ROBERT LOUIS STEVENSON

"Sir, we had a good talk."—JOHNSON.

"As we must account for every idle word, so we must for every idle silence."—FRANKLIN.

There can be no fairer ambition than to excel in talk; to be affable, gay, ready, clear and welcome; to have a fact, a thought, or an illustration, pat to every subject; and not only to cheer the flight of time among our intimates, but bear our part in that great international congress, always sitting, where public wrongs are first declared, public errors first corrected, and the course of public opinion shaped, day by day, a little nearer to the right. No measure comes before Parliament but it has been long ago prepared by the grand jury of the talkers; no book is written that has not been largely composed by their assistance. Literature in many of its branches is no other than the shadow of good talk; but the imitation falls far short of the original in life, freedom, and effect. There are always two to a talk, giving and taking, comparing experience and according conclusions. Talk is fluid, tentative, continually "in further search and progress;" while written words remain fixed, become idols even to the writer, found wooden dogmatisms, and preserve flies of obvious error in the amber of the truth. Last and chief, while literature, gagged with linsey-woolsey, can only deal with a fraction of the life of man, talk goes fancy free and may call a spade a spade. It cannot, even if it would, become merely aesthetic or merely classical like literature. A jest intervenes, the solemn humbug is dissolved in laughter, and speech runs forth out of the contemporary groove into the open fields of nature, cheery and cheering, like schoolboys out of school. And it is in talk alone that we can learn our period and ourselves. In short, the first duty of a man is to speak; that is his chief business in this world; and talk, which is the harmonious speech of two or more, is by far the most accessible of pleasures. It costs nothing in money; it is all profit; it completes our education, founds and fosters our friendships, and can be enjoyed at any age and in almost any state of health.

The spice of life is battle; the friendliest relations are still a kind of contest; and if we would not forego all that is valuable in our lot, we must continually face some other person, eye to eye, and wrestle a fall whether in love or enmity. It is still by force of body, or power of character or intellect, that we attain to worthy pleasures. Men and women contend for each other in the lists of love, like rival mesmerists; the active and adroit decide their challenges in the sports of the body; and the sedentary sit down to chess or conversation. All sluggish and pacific pleasures are, to the same degree, solitary and selfish; and every durable bond between human beings is founded in or heightened by some element of competition. Now, the relation that has the least root in matter is undoubtedly that airy one of friendship; and hence, I suppose, it is that good talk most commonly arises among friends. Talk is, indeed, both the scene and instrument of friendship. It is in talk alone that the friends can measure strength, and enjoy that amicable counter-assertion of personality which is the gauge of relations and the sport of life.

A good talk is not to be had for the asking. Humours must first be accorded in a kind of overture or prologue; hour, company and circumstance be suited; and then, at a fit juncture, the subject, the quarry of two heated minds, springs up like a deer out of the wood. Not that the talker has any of the hunter's pride, though he has all and more than all his ardour. The genuine artist follows the stream of conversation as an angler follows the windings of a brook, not dallying where he fails to "kill." He trusts implicitly to hazard; and he is rewarded by continual variety, continual pleasure, and those changing prospects of the truth that are the best of education. There is nothing in a subject, so called, that we should regard it as an idol, or follow it beyond the promptings of desire. Indeed, there are few subjects; and so far as they are truly talkable, more than the half of them may be reduced to three: that I am I, that you are you, and that there are other people dimly understood to be not quite the same as either. Wherever talk may range, it still runs half the time on these eternal lines. The theme being set, each plays on himself as on an instrument; asserts and justifies himself; ransacks his brain for instances and opinions, and brings them forth new-minted, to his own surprise and the admiration of his adversary. All natural talk is a festival of ostentation; and by the laws of the game each accepts and fans the vanity of the other. It is from that reason that we venture to lay ourselves so open, that we dare to be so warmly eloquent, and that we swell in each other's eyes to such a vast proportion. For talkers, once launched, begin to overflow the limits of their ordinary selves, tower up to the height of their secret pretensions, and give themselves out for the heroes, brave, pious, musical, and wise, that in their most shining moments they aspire to be. So they weave for themselves with words and for a while inhabit a palace of delights, temple at once and theatre, where they fill the round of the world's dignities, and feast with the gods, exulting in Kudos.[39] And when the talk is over, each goes his way, still flushed with vanity and admiration, still trailing clouds of glory; each declines from the height of his ideal orgy, not in a moment, but by slow declension. I remember, in the *entr'acte* of an afternoon performance, coming forth into the sunshine, in a beautiful green, gardened corner of a romantic city; and as I sat and smoked, the music moving in my blood, I seemed to sit there and evaporate *The Flying Dutchman* (for it was that I had been hearing) with a wonderful sense of life, warmth, well-being, and pride; and the noises of the city, voices, bells and marching feet, fell together in my ears like a symphonious orchestra. In the same way, the excitement of a good talk lives for a long while after in the blood, the heart still hot within you, the brain still simmering, and the physical earth swimming around you with the colours of the sunset.

Natural talk, like ploughing, should turn up a large surface of life, rather than dig mines into geological strata. Masses of experience, anecdote, incident, cross-lights, quotation, historical instances, the whole flotsam and jetsam of two minds forced in and in upon the matter in hand from every point of the compass, and from every degree of mental elevation and abasement—these are the material with which talk is fortified, the food on which the talkers thrive. Such argument as is proper to the exercise should still be brief and seizing. Talk should proceed by instances; by the apposite, not the expository. It should keep close along the lines of humanity, near the bosoms and businesses of men, at the level where history, fiction and experience intersect and illuminate each other. I am I, and You are You, with all my heart; but conceive how these lean propositions change and brighten when, instead of words, the actual you and I sit cheek by jowl, the spirit housed in the live body, and the very clothes uttering voices to corroborate the story in the face. Not less surprising is the change when we leave off to speak of generalities—the bad, the good, the miser, and all the characters of Theophrastus—and call up other men, by anecdote or instance, in their very trick and feature; or trading on a common knowledge, toss each other famous names, still glowing with the hues of life. Communication is no longer by words, but by the instancing of whole biographies, epics, systems of philosophy, and epochs of history, in bulk.

That which is understood excels that which is spoken in quantity and quality alike; ideas thus figured and personified, change hands, as we may say, like coin; and the speakers imply without effort the most obscure and intricate thoughts. Strangers who have a large common ground of reading will, for this reason, come the sooner to the grapple of genuine converse. If they know Othello and Napoleon, Consuelo and Clarissa Harlowe, Vautrin and Steenie Steenson, they can leave generalities and begin at once to speak by figures.

Conduct and art are the two subjects that arise most frequently and that embrace the widest range of facts. A few pleasures bear discussion for their own sake, but only those which are most social or most radically human; and even these can only be discussed among their devotees. A technicality is always welcome to the expert, whether in athletics, art, or law; I have heard the best kind of talk on technicalities from such rare and happy persons as both know and love their business. No human being ever spoke of scenery for above two minutes at a time, which makes me suspect we hear too much of it in literature. The weather is regarded as the very nadir and scoff of conversational topics. And yet the weather, the dramatic element in scenery, is far more tractable in language, and far more human both in import and suggestion than the stable features of the landscape. Sailors and shepherds, and the people generally of coast and mountain, talk well of it; and it is often excitingly presented in literature. But the tendency of all living talk draws it back and back into the common focus of humanity. Talk is a creature of the street and market-place, feeding on gossip; and its last resort is still in a discussion on morals. That is the heroic form of gossip; heroic in virtue of its high pretensions; but still gossip, because it turns on personalities. You can keep no men long, nor Scotchmen at all, off moral or theological discussion. These are to all the world what law is to lawyers; they are everybody's technicalities; the medium through which all consider life, and the dialect in which they express their judgments. I knew three young men who walked together daily for some two months in a solemn and beautiful forest and in cloudless summer weather; daily they talked with unabated zest, and yet scarce wandered that whole time beyond two subjects—theology and love. And perhaps neither a court of love[40] nor an assembly of divines would have granted their premises or welcomed their conclusions.

Conclusions, indeed, are not often reached by talk any more than by private thinking. That is not the profit. The profit is in the exercise, and above all in the experience; for when we reason at large on any subject, we review our state and history in life. From time to time, however, and specially, I think, in talking art, talk becomes effective, conquering like war, widening the boundaries of knowledge like an exploration. A point arises; the question takes a problematical, a baffling, yet a likely air; the talkers begin to feel lively presentiments of some conclusion near at hand; towards this they strive with emulous ardour, each by his own path, and struggling for first utterance; and then one leaps upon the summit of that matter with a shout, and almost at the same moment the other is beside him; and behold they are agreed. Like enough, the progress is illusory, a mere cat's cradle having been wound and unwound out of words. But the sense of joint discovery is none the less giddy and inspiring. And in the life of the talker such triumphs, though imaginary, are neither few nor far apart; they are attained with speed and pleasure, in the hour of mirth; and by the nature of the process, they are always worthily shared.

There is a certain attitude combative at once and deferential, eager to fight yet most averse to quarrel, which marks out at once the talkable man. It is not eloquence, not fairness, not obstinacy, but a certain proportion of all of these that I love to encounter in my amicable adversaries. They must not be pontiffs holding doctrine, but huntsmen questing after elements of truth. Neither must they be boys to be instructed, but fellow-teachers with whom I may wrangle and agree on equal terms. We must reach some solution, some shadow of consent; for without that, eager talk becomes a torture. But we do not wish to reach it cheaply, or quickly, or without the tussle and effort Wherein pleasure lies.

The very best talker, with me, is one whom I shall call Spring-Heel'd Jack. I say so, because I never knew any one who mingled so largely the possible ingredients of converse. In the Spanish proverb, the fourth man necessary to compound a salad, is a madman to mix it: Jack is that madman. I know not which is more remarkable: the insane lucidity of his conclusions, the humorous eloquence of his language, or his power of method, bringing the whole of life into the focus of the subject treated, mixing the conversational salad like a drunken god. He doubles like the serpent, changes and flashes like the shaken kaleidoscope, transmigrates bodily into the views of others, and so, in the twinkling of an eye and with a heady rapture, turns questions inside out and flings them empty before you on the ground, like a triumphant conjuror. It is my common practice when a piece of conduct puzzles me, to attack it in the presence of Jack with such grossness, such partiality and such wearing iteration, as at length shall spur him up in its defence. In a moment he transmigrates, dons the required character, and with moonstruck philosophy justifies the act in question. I can fancy nothing to compare with the *vim* of these impersonations, the strange scale of language, flying from Shakespeare to Kant, and from Kant to Major Dyngwell—

"As fast as a musician scatters sounds
Out of an instrument—"

the sudden, sweeping generalisations, the absurd irrelevant particularities, the wit, wisdom, folly, humour, eloquence and bathos, each startling in its kind, and yet all luminous in the admired disorder of their combination. A talker of a different calibre, though belonging to the same school, is Burly. Burly is a man of great presence; he commands a larger atmosphere, gives the impression of a grosser mass of character than most men. It has been said of him that his presence could be felt in a room you entered blindfold; and the same, I think, has been said of other powerful constitutions condemned to much physical inaction. There is something boisterous and piratic in Burly's manner of talk which suits well enough with this impression. He will roar you down, he will bury his face in his hands, he will undergo passions of revolt and agony; and meanwhile his attitude of mind is really both conciliatory and receptive; and after Pistol has been out-Pistol'd, and the welkin rung for hours, you begin to perceive a certain subsidence in these spring torrents, points of agreement issue, and you end arm-in-arm, and in a glow of mutual admiration. The outcry only serves to make your final union the more unexpected and precious. Throughout there has been perfect sincerity, perfect intelligence, a desire to hear although not always to listen, and an unaffected eagerness to meet concessions. You have, with Burly, none of the dangers that attend debate with Spring-Heel'd Jack; who may at any moment turn his powers of transmigration on yourself, create for you a view you never held, and then furiously fall on you for holding it. These, at least, are my two favourites, and both are loud, copious, intolerant talkers. This argues that I myself am in the same category; for if we love talking at all, we love a bright, fierce adversary, who will hold his ground, foot by foot, in much our own manner, sell his attention dearly, and give us our full measure of the dust and exertion of battle. Both these men can be beat from a position, but it takes six hours to do it; a high and hard adventure, worth attempting. With both you can pass days in an enchanted country of the mind, with people, scenery and manners of its own; live a life apart, more arduous, active and glowing than any real existence; and come forth again when the talk is over, as out of a theatre or a dream, to find the east wind still blowing and the chimney-pots of the old battered city still around you. Jack has the far finer mind, Burly the far more honest; Jack gives us the animated poetry, Burly the romantic prose, of similar themes; the one glances high like a meteor and makes a light in darkness; the other, with many changing hues of fire, burns at the sea-level, like a conflagration; but both have the same humour and artistic interests, the same unquenched ardour in pursuit, the same gusts of talk and thunderclaps of contradiction.

Cockshot[41] is a different article, but vastly entertaining, and has been meat and drink to me for many a long evening. His manner is dry, brisk and pertinacious, and the choice of words not much. The point about him is his extraordinary readiness and spirit. You can propound nothing but he has either a theory about it ready-made, or will have one instantly on the stocks, and proceed to lay its timbers and launch it in your presence. "Let me see," he will say. "Give me a moment. I *should* have some theory for that." A blither spectacle than the vigour with which he sets about the task, it were hard to fancy. He is possessed by a demoniac energy, welding the elements for his life, and bending ideas, as an athlete bends a horseshoe, with a visible and lively effort. He has, in theorising, a compass, an art; what I would call the synthetic gusto; something of a Herbert Spencer, who should see the fun of the thing. You are not bound, and no more is he, to place your faith in these brand-new opinions. But some of them are right enough, durable even for life; and the poorest serve for a cock-shy—as when idle people, after picnics, float a bottle on a pond and have an hour's diversion ere, it sinks. Whichever they are, serious opinions or humours of the moment, he still defends his ventures with indefatigable wit and spirit, hitting savagely himself, but taking punishment like a man. He knows and never forgets that people talk, first of all, for the sake of talking; conducts himself in the ring, to use the old slang, like a thorough "glutton," and honestly enjoys a telling facer from his adversary. Cockshot is bottled effervescency, the sworn foe of sleep. Three-in-the-morning Cockshot, says a victim. His talk is like the driest of all imaginable dry champagnes. Sleight of hand and inimitable quickness are the qualities by which he lives. Athelred, on the other hand, presents you with the spectacle of a sincere and somewhat slow nature thinking aloud. He is the most unready man I ever knew to shine in conversation. You may see him sometimes wrestle with a refractory jest for a minute or two together, and perhaps fail to throw it in the end. And there is something singularly engaging, often instructive, in the simplicity with which he thus exposes the process as well as the result, the works as well as the dial of the clock. Withal he has his hours of inspiration. Apt words come to him as if by accident, and, coming from deeper down, they smack the more personally, they have the more of fine old crusted humanity, rich in sediment and humour. There are sayings of his in which he has stamped himself into the very grain of the language; you would think he must have worn the words next his skin and slept with them. Yet it is not as a sayer of particular good things that Athelred is most to be regarded, rather as the stalwart woodman of thought. I have pulled on a light cord often enough, while he has been wielding the broad-axe; and between us, on this unequal, division, many a specious fallacy has fallen. I have known him to battle the same question night after night for years, keeping it in the reign of talk, constantly applying it and re-applying it to life with humorous or grave intention, and all the while, never hurrying, nor flagging, nor taking an unfair advantage of the facts. Jack at a given moment, when arising, as it were, from the tripod, can be more radiantly just to those from whom he differs; but then the tenor of his thoughts is even calumnious; while Athelred, slower to forge excuses, is yet slower to condemn, and sits over the welter of the world, vacillating but still judicial, and still faithfully contending with his doubts.

Both the last talkers deal much in points of conduct and religion studied in the "dry light" of prose. Indirectly and as if against his will the same elements from time to time appear in the troubled and poetic talk of

Opalstein. His various and exotic knowledge, complete although unready sympathies, and fine, full, discriminative flow of language, fit him out to be the best of talkers; so perhaps he is with some, not *quite* with me—*proxime accessit*,[42] I should say. He sings the praises of the earth and the arts, flowers and jewels, wine and music, in a moonlight, serenading manner, as to the light guitar; even wisdom comes from his tongue like singing; no one is, indeed, more tuneful in the upper notes. But even while he sings the song of the Sirens, he still hearkens to the barking of the Sphinx. Jarring Byronic notes interrupt the flow of his Horatian humours. His mirth has something of the tragedy of the world for its perpetual background; and he feasts like Don Giovanni to a double orchestra, one lightly sounding for the dance, one pealing Beethoven in the distance. He is not truly reconciled either with life or with himself; and this instant war in his members sometimes divides the man's attention. He does not always, perhaps not often, frankly surrender himself in conversation. He brings into the talk other thoughts than those which he expresses; you are conscious that he keeps an eye on something else, that he does not shake off the world, nor quite forget himself. Hence arise occasional disappointments; even an occasional unfairness for his companions, who find themselves one day giving too much, and the next, when they are wary out of season, giving perhaps too little. Purcel is in another class from any I have mentioned. He is no debater, but appears in conversation, as occasion rises, in two distinct characters, one of which I admire and fear, and the other love. In the first, he is radiantly civil and rather silent, sits on a high, courtly hilltop, and from that vantage-ground drops you his remarks like favours. He seems not to share in our sublunary contentions; he wears no sign of interest; when on a sudden there falls in a crystal of wit, so polished that the dull do not perceive it, but so right that the sensitive are silenced. True talk should have more body and blood, should be louder, vainer and more declaratory of the man; the true talker should not hold so steady an advantage over whom he speaks with; and that is one reason out of a score why I prefer my Purcel in his second character, when he unbends into a strain of graceful gossip, singing like the fireside kettle. In these moods he has an elegant homeliness that rings of the true Queen Anne. I know another person who attains, in his moments, to the insolence of a Restoration comedy, speaking, I declare, as Congreve wrote; but that is a sport of nature, and scarce falls under the rubric, for there is none, alas! to give him answer.

One last remark occurs: It is the mark of genuine conversation that the sayings can scarce be quoted with their full effect beyond the circle of common friends. To have their proper weight they, should appear in a biography, and with the portrait of the speaker. Good talk is dramatic; it is like an impromptu piece of acting where each should represent himself to the greatest advantage; and that is the best kind of talk where each speaker is most fully and candidly himself, and where, if you were to shift the speeches, round from one to another, there would be the greatest loss in significance and perspicuity. It is for this reason that talk depends so wholly on our company. We should like to introduce Falstaff and Mercutio, or Falstaff and Sir Toby; but Falstaff in talk with Cordelia seems even painful. Most of us, by the Protean quality of man, can talk to some degree with all; but the true talk, that strikes out all the slumbering best of us, comes only with the peculiar brethren of our spirits, is founded as deep as love in the constitution of our being, and is a thing to relish with all our energy, while yet we have it, and to be grateful for forever.

FOOTNOTES:

[Footnote 38: The first of two papers on this subject written in 1881-2; reprinted here, by permission of the publishers, from "Memories and Portraits" in the Biographical Edition of Stevenson's Works, Charles Scribner's Sons, 1907.]

[Footnote 39: Kudos (Greek): glory.]

[Footnote 40: Court of love: a mediaeval institution for the discussion of questions of chivalry.]

[Footnote 41: The Late Fleeming Jenkin—Author's note.]

[Footnote 42: Proxime accessit: he comes very close to it.]

www.ingramcontent.com/pod-product-compliance
Lightning Source LLC
Chambersburg PA
CBHW081108080526

44587CB00021B/3506